# Poverty in Scotland

# 2002

## People, places and policies

**Edited by: Usha Brown, Gill Scott,
Gerry Mooney, Bryony Duncan**

CPAG • 94 White Lion Street • London N1 9PF

CPAG promotes action for the relief, directly or indirectly, of poverty among children and families with children. We work to ensure that those on low incomes get their full entitlements to welfare benefits. In our campaigning and information work we seek to improve benefits and policies for low-income families in order to eradicate the injustice of poverty. If you are not already supporting us, please consider making a donation, or ask for details of our membership schemes and publications.

Poverty Publication 106

Published by CPAG in association with the Scottish Poverty Information Unit

© CPAG/Scottish Poverty Information Unit 2002

ISBN 1 901698 50 5

The views expressed in this book are the authors' and do not necessarily express those of CPAG or the Scottish Poverty Information Unit.

A CIP record for this book is available from the British Library

Cover and design by Devious Designs 0114 2755634, based on an original design by John Gahagan
Typeset by Boldface 020 7253 2014
Printed by Russell Press 0115 9784505

# About the publishers

**CPAG in Scotland** is part of CPAG and works to promote action for the relief, directly or indirectly, of poverty among children and families with children. We work to ensure that those on low incomes get their full entitlements to welfare benefits. In our campaigning and information work we seek to improve benefits and policies for low-income families in order to eradicate the injustice of poverty. If you are not already supporting us, please consider making a donation, or ask for details of membership schemes and publications.

**The Scottish Poverty Information Unit, based at Glasgow Caledonian University**, provides an information and research service on poverty in Scotland to those working in the anti-poverty field, in order to enable organisations and groups to combat poverty more effectively. The Unit has a commitment to work with others to tackle poverty by: providing accurate and accessible information on poverty and social exclusion in Scotland; delivering research expertise to communities; supporting interest in, and debate and discussion on, poverty and poverty-related issues; disseminating information as widely as possible.

# About the contributors

**Usha Brown** (Editor) is a research fellow at the Scottish Poverty Information Unit, Glasgow Caledonian University.

**Linda Croxford** is a lecturer at the Centre for Educational Sociology, University of Edinburgh.

**Bryony Duncan** (Editor) is a research fellow at the Scottish Poverty Information Unit, Glasgow Caledonian University.

**Iain Ferguson** is a lecturer in the Department of Applied Social Science, University of Stirling.

**Rona Fitzgerald** is a research fellow at the European Policies Research Centre.

**Morag Gillespie** is Director of Citizens Rights and Advice, Fife.

**Sue Laughlin** is a senior policy worker in health services.

**Leaza McSorley** is a researcher at the School of Economics and Enterprise, Glasgow Caledonian University.

**Gerry Mooney** (Editor) is a senior lecturer in social policy at the Open University.

**Danny Phillips** is Child Poverty Action Group in Scotland's policy officer.

**Gill Scott** (Editor) is Director of the Scottish Poverty Information Unit, Glasgow Caledonian University.

**John Wilson** is Director of the Scottish Low Pay Unit.

# Contents

**Section one: Introduction**

1   **The changing context**                           3

**Section two: Poverty in Scotland 2002**

2   **Definitions, measurements and
    incidence of poverty**                            11

3   **Factors leading to poverty**                    33

4   **Groups vulnerable to poverty**                  57

5   **Living with poverty**                           88

**Section three: People, places and policies**

6   **Child poverty in Scotland**                     97

7   **Social policy and family poverty**             103

8   **Local areas and regeneration**                 108

9   **Equalities and poverty**                        113

10  **Poverty and asylum seekers**                    118

11  **Poverty and welfare**                           124

12  **Poverty and low pay**                           129

13  **The New Deal**                                  133

14  **From the public to the private?**               139

15 **The effects of poverty on early**     144
   **education – findings from the Early**
   **Intervention Programme in Scotland**

16 **Health policy in Scotland since 1997**     151
   **and its impact on poverty**

**Section four: Conclusions**

17 **Continuities and contradictions**     157

Appendix one: **Suggestions for further**     165
   **reading**

Appendix two: **Information sources**     168

Appendix three: **Policy diary**     170

# Acknowledgements

We are very grateful to all the people who contributed to this book. Their enthusiasm for mapping poverty, and highlighting major issues in current policy directions was much appreciated. Special thanks must go to Adrian Sinfield, Gil Long and Les Brown for their comments on the draft manuscript. Their advice and assistance was invaluable from beginning to end.

For information and advice we would like to thank Irfan Arif, David Brownlee, Marian Davis, Bob Downes, Alan Fleming, Simon Fraser, Morag Gillespie, Julie Goodal, Ginny Jackson, Ian Hertwick, Jacqueline Kelly, Alistair Mckinley, Bill Scott, Kay Sillars, Emily Thompson and Steve Topping.

Thanks are also due to the agencies in which they work: Age Concern Scotland, Citizens Advice Bureau (Parkhead), Central Statistics Unit, Scottish Executive, CPAG Scotland, Commission for Racial Equality, Communities Scotland, Department of Public Health, Women's Health Greater Glasgow NHS Trust, DWP Analytic Services Division, Department for Work and Pensions, Job Centre Plus (Office for Scotland), One Plus, Poverty Alliance and the Social Inclusion Division of the Scottish Executive.

Finally, the editors would like to thank colleagues in Glasgow Caledonian University and the Open University for their support.

# Section one
## Introduction

# One
# The changing context

This is the fourth edition of *Poverty in Scotland*. Each edition updates and expands the information provided by the previous one. The books originated in a lack of reliable and accessible information on poverty in Scotland. Since the last one was published (*Poverty in Scotland* 1999) there have been a number of developments. One of the most important was the re-establishment of a Scottish Parliament in May 1999. This promised to promote distinctively Scottish ways of addressing poverty and social exclusion. In addition, there is now a range of geographically specific anti-poverty measures, and more Scottish poverty statistics (for example, the Scottish Household Survey and the boosted Family Resource Survey).

This section provides a brief overview of the context in which this book was written, some of the key themes in current anti-poverty policy, and a summary of the structure of the book.

## Labour: tackling poverty

In 1997 the Labour Government was elected to power. The new government made strong commitments to combating poverty and in particular child poverty:

> 'Our historic aim will be for ours to be the first generation to end child poverty, and it will take a generation. It is a twenty-year mission, but I believe it can be done.'[1]

Before the 1997 election, Tony Blair stated that if Labour did not effectively tackle the problems of poverty it would have failed.

Labour's willingness to resurrect the concept of poverty, and to locate anti-poverty policies high on the political agenda for the first time in decades, represented a major sea change from the approach of past Conservative governments. Action already taken includes real rises in child benefits, various minimum income guarantees, a commitment to develop a childcare and early years strategy, the introduction of a national minimum wage, a series of tax and benefit reforms, and a wide and diverse range of other measures that both directly and indirectly relate to poverty in the fields of health, education, housing, neighbourhood renewal and crime prevention.

## The Third Way

Radical rethinking of many of its key concepts supported the push for electoral success by the Labour Party. The new government made it clear that it would adopt a pragmatic approach, focusing on policies and solutions (regardless of their place in the political spectrum) that would address the problems the country faced and improve people's lives – the 'Third Way'.

The idea of a Third Way has been the subject of much debate and speculation. It is underpinned by the argument that both the 'tax and spend', nationalising and state interventionist policies of 'old' Labour, as well as the market-driven policies of the Conservatives, failed fundamentally to tackle poverty and disadvantage in Britain. Against these 'two failed pasts', New Labour seeks to construct an approach that is in line with recent economic and social developments, both in Britain and internationally. It argues that it is an approach that will take into account: changes in family structure and demographic profile in Britain; the new conditions of globalisation; and the need to transform Britain into a fit, healthy, knowledge-based economy, with a flexible, well-educated and highly skilled workforce.

In addition the Third Way embraces the view that in the context of globalisation the role of the state, both nationally and internationally, has been modified. All of these factors, it is claimed, necessitate a new approach to welfare and to social policy in general.

Policy on poverty in this new approach has a number of strands. Key ones are: a re-analysis of poverty as social exclusion; a focus on child poverty; work as the favoured route out of poverty; modernisation of the welfare state (in particular social security); area-based poverty strategies; stress on the obligations owed by individuals to community and state in return for the rights conferred by welfare provision.

## Social exclusion

Attempts to construct a new Third Way approach in general, and the goal of modernising the welfare state in particular, have helped to shape the Labour Government's approach to poverty. The Government accepted the existence of income poverty, but felt that issues of disadvantage were wider, and it promoted the use of the concept social exclusion. This, it was felt, represented the more dynamic and wide-ranging processes and relationships involved:

> 'Social exclusion is not just about poverty, but about living in neighbourhoods that are crime-ridden and lack access to shops, transport, decent schooling and job opportunities.'[2]

There was an implicit promise in the notion to examine all of the processes contributing to poverty, including, for example, racism and sexism. But the Government also made it clear that its concerns were with social exclusion and poverty, not inequality. Policies were aimed at increasing equality of opportunities, not equality of outcome.

## From welfare to work

The Labour Government's plans for large-scale reform of the welfare state, in particular social security, have given way to smaller incremental changes. Even so, the central role of 'work' in its policy remains. Social exclusion is largely defined as exclusion from work – as paid employment – and, in turn, social inclusion is principally dependent upon entering paid employment.

There is now an explicit tying of social security to the labour market. The aim is to create a social security system which will ensure 'work for those who can and security for those who cannot'. Enabling people to find work and ensuring that work pays will, in the Government's view, both help them out of poverty and reduce the social security bill. The introduction of the national minimum wage, the curtailing of many benefits and the extension of targeting and means-testing play an important role in encouraging those on benefit to take up work. Additionally, a range of measures has been introduced to improve employability through education and training.

An indication of the shape of current reform was the re-naming, in July 2001, of the Department of Social Security as the Department for Work and Pensions. A single service now has responsibility for employment, equal opportunities, benefits, pensions and child support.

## New Labour and welfare: rights and responsibilities

Debate about the future of welfare in Britain has become increasingly focused on morality, behaviour and personal character. In important respects, Labour's welfare reforms have been as much about forging fundamental changes in the relationship between the individual and the state, as they have been about developing new ways of tackling poverty or social exclusion.

The language of, and stress upon, 'responsibilities' and 'duties' has come to be a consistent feature of many of Labour's social and welfare policies. In turn, this is linked to the idea of the 'greater good': that individuals have important duties to family, community and to society as a whole. For those who seek to side-step their social responsibilities, there is a range of penalties as in, for example, the withdrawal of benefits for those neglecting to take up work.

## The Scottish Parliament

'Too many Scots are excluded, by virtue of unemployment, low skills levels, poverty, bad health, poor housing or other factors, from full participation in society. Those of us who benefit from the opportunities of life in modern Scotland have a duty to seek to extend similar opportunities to those who do not. Social exclusion is unacceptable in human terms; it is also wasteful, costly and carries risks in the long term for our social cohesion and well-being. This government is determined to take action to tackle exclusion, and to develop policies, which will promote a more inclusive, cohesive and ultimately sustainable society.'[3]

Tackling poverty and social exclusion were also seen as a major priority for the re-established Scottish Parliament in Edinburgh. The Scottish Parliament has wide powers over most domestic matters affecting Scotland, including many of the key social policy areas of housing, health, education and social work. But Westminster retains control over three key policy areas that relate to poverty and social exclusion – social security, employment policy and taxes. These are not insignificant. Policies to tackle worklessness and changes in the benefits system have major effects on the lives of those living in poverty.

Since 1999 the Scottish Executive has sought to present the attack on poverty as a central organising principle of the new Parliament. In some important respects this has involved a degree of divergence between Holyrood and Westminster. While it should not be overstated, nonetheless it is also significant that a different language is often mobilised in Scotland. Thus there is a greater stress on social inclusion (as opposed to exclusion), on partnership, equality and, importantly, on social justice. There is now a Minister of Social Justice with responsibility for these issues.

## Structure of the book

This new edition brings most of the relevant data up to date and includes many new Scottish sources. In addition, there are a series of short essays that provide informed and critical analyses of the UK government's and the Scottish Executive's record in tackling poverty since devolution.

It should be noted that this book does not provide an exhaustive survey of all aspects of poverty in Scotland. There are a number of subjects that are not covered and others that are only covered briefly. Limitations of space and time meant that we have had to be selective, and have chosen to concentrate on the less publicised structural information. The policy essays do not cover all areas or aspects of any issue. They are short discussions intended to raise matters of interest or concern. Opinions in the essays are those of contributors and do not necessarily represent the views of the Scottish Poverty Information Unit, nor of the editors.

The rest of the book is in three sections:

### Section 2: Poverty in Scotland 2002
An update of information in previous editions.

### Section 3: People, places and policies
This section contains a range of individual contributions from political, academic and voluntary sectors in Scotland. Contributors were asked to con-

sider: the relationship between government policy and poverty; the effectiveness of policy in combating poverty; and possible future directions. All contributors are in a position to comment in an informed way on the particularities and similarities of Scotland's experience of poverty and the policy responses. They bring an authoritative voice to the assessment of how national and regional economic factors affect the responses to poverty in Scotland.

## Section 4: Conclusions

The final section considers the key themes raised by information and policy responses in the book.

## Notes

1   T Blair, 'Beveridge Revisited: a welfare state for the twenty-first century', speech at Toynbee Hall, 18 March 1999
2   A Giddens, 'There is No Alternative: the Third Way is the only way forward', *The Independent*, 8 January 2002
3   Donald Dewar, reported in *The Herald*, 3 February 1998

# Section two

# Poverty in Scotland 2002

# Definitions, measurements and incidence of poverty

Ideas about poverty are complex, often contradictory and influenced by factors such as personal experiences, value judgements and belief systems. Inevitably definitions of poverty are contested. There is no single, universally accepted definition.

## Absolute and relative poverty

The two most commonly used definitions of poverty are 'absolute' and 'relative' poverty. The Scottish Executive and the UK government also use the terms 'social exclusion' and 'social justice' in their discussion of poverty.

Absolute poverty refers to the level of resources needed to sustain physical survival. People are poor if they cannot feed, cloth or house themselves and their dependants. However, the resources needed for survival and the ways in which they are acquired change with time and location. Moreover, as people's lives change, the necessities they require also change:

'An adequate minimum is itself defined by what is socially acceptable.'[1]

Relative poverty is defined in relation to the standards of living in a society at a particular time. People live in poverty when they are denied an income sufficient for their material needs, and when these circumstances exclude them from taking part in activities that are an accepted part of daily life in that society. One problem with this definition is that in an affluent society it could become difficult to distinguish between those who are poor and those who are just less well off; some commentators argue that relative definitions necessarily refer to inequality, not poverty. Despite its shortcomings, in this book we use the relative measure of poverty, believing that poverty should be defined by the standards of society as it is today.

## Social exclusion

Definitions of social exclusion usually describe how and why it occurs, as well as its implications. The European Union notes that social exclusion occurs when people cannot fully participate or contribute to society because of 'the denial of civil, political, social, economic and cultural rights'.[2] Definitions also indicate that it results from 'a combination of linked problems such as unemployment, poor skills, low incomes, poor housing, bad health and family breakdown'.[3] The term is useful in encompassing the multi-dimensional nature of poverty, and examining the complex relationship between causes and effects of poverty.

## Social justice

Social justice is a broad and contested term. Definitions vary across the political spectrum; they include ideas of distributive justice, utilitarian themes, equality, and libertarian ideas of 'governance'. The Commission on Social Justice, set up in 1992 by the late John Smith, the leader of the Labour Party at that time, to carry out an independent enquiry into economic and social reform, noted that 'our view of social justice consists of four key ideas'. These were: equal worth of all citizens; citizens' entitlement to be able to meet their basic needs; the widest possible spread of opportunities; and the reduction or elimination of unjust inequalities.[4] Although the Scottish Executive uses the term social justice, it does not define it. It is used to cover the Executive's commitment to tackling poverty and disadvantage, rebuilding and strengthening our communities, and increasing opportunity for all through education.

Roll points out that a drawback of a very broad approach is that issues of deprivation and disadvantage are concealed within broader social questions, and this can result in the definitions of poverty becoming confused with its explanations.[5] Discrimination, for example, is a major cause of poverty, but discrimination does not necessarily imply poverty; many who face discrimination are not poor. Moreover, very broad approaches are difficult both to measure and to evaluate.

Much of this debate can be set aside if the search for a unitary definition is abandoned and it is recognised that there are different degrees and dimensions of poverty.[6] Debates about poverty definitions should not obscure what it means to those who experience it. The distinctions and debates about definitions are largely irrelevant to those who live with the limitations that inadequate incomes impose.

## Measurement and incidence of poverty

The way we calculate the number of people who live in poverty has become very technical and can be off-putting. The situation is complicated by the fact that in Britain there has been no official poverty line. A variety of different methods are used to assess levels of poverty in Britain. As a consequence, there is a mass of complex data available about the extent of poverty that is not always compatible, and can be difficult to interpret. Nevertheless, two commonly used measures are the *Households Below Average Income* series and the numbers of people claiming the social security benefit, income support.

### Households Below Average Income

*Households Below Average Income* (HBAI) is an annual review of income distribution compiled by the Department for Work and Pensions (previously the Department of Social Security). It was first published in 1988; the latest edition published in April 2002 covers the period between 1994/95 and 2000/01. It is a major source of information on people living on low incomes and provides 'an explicitly relative measure which looks at how people at the bottom of the income distribution have fared in relation to the average'.[7]

HBAI provides official figures on low income. In the past, 50 per cent of *mean* net income was used as the income poverty measure; it is still widely used. In 1998 the Statistical Program Committee of the European Union (EU) decided that 60 per cent of *median* income should be used as the measure of income poverty when making international comparisons. This is now the favoured measure of the British government. It should be noted that the EU Committee also recommended that other thresholds (for example 40, 50 and 70 per cent of the median and mean) should also be used when considering poverty, in order to obtain the fullest picture.

Mean and median refer to different ways of measuring the average.

The mean is most commonly used as the average. Mean income is found by adding all the incomes of a population and dividing the result by the number of people in that population. But the measure can easily be distorted by very low or very high income figures. The median refers to the mid-point of a given set of figures. This measure is less susceptible to distortions and therefore more reliable. The 60 per cent median threshold was chosen because it is within the same range as the 50 per cent mean.

It should be noted that the adequacy of these income poverty thresholds has not been established and, therefore, we do not know if the incomes they represent actually keep people out of poverty.[8]

Two measures are used in HBAI series: net income before housing costs, and net income after housing costs. In this publication the 'after housing cost' measure is used, because for families on low incomes, housing costs represent a fixed budget item over which they have little choice. Moreover, housing expenditure varies widely across the country and at different life stages. It should be noted that Scotland has a higher proportion of people using public sector housing and a smaller private rented sector than the rest of the UK.

Table 2.1 shows the money value of 50 per cent mean and 60 per cent median income measures (after housing costs), for different family types.

Table 2.1

**The poverty line in 2000/01 defined as both 50 per cent mean and 60 per cent median net income (after housing costs and including self-employed)**
**£ per week, UK**

| Family type | 50% mean | 60% median |
|---|---|---|
| Single with no children | 87 | 84 |
| Couple with no children | 158 | 153 |
| Single with two children (aged 5 and 11) | 161 | 156 |
| Couple with two children (aged 5 and 11) | 232 | 225 |
| **All family types** | **158** | **153** |

Source: Department for Work and Pensions, *Households Below Average Income*, 2000/01, 2002, Table 2.2

## Income support

Income support is a means-tested benefit for people whose income falls below a specified level, or who have no other source of income. This may be because they are retired or unable to work because they are sick, disabled, pregnant or caring for others. The amount paid is dependent on family size and type, with extra amounts added for certain claimant groups, for example, disabled people, carers and pensioners. Income-based jobseeker's allowance replaced income support for unemployed people in 1996. It is a means-tested benefit paid to people registered as available for and actively seeking work, whose incomes fall below a specified level.

There are people who live on incomes at or below the level of income support and *need* benefits but do not receive them, either because they do not *qualify* for them, or because they do not *claim* them and they will not be included in the claimant count. For these reasons and because changes in eligibility criteria can trigger changes in the number of people defined as living in poverty, some commentators claim that benefit rates may not be reliable measures of poverty. Nevertheless, the level of income support represents a crude official indication of the minimum income required for living in Britain today: it is, in effect, a poverty line.

Table 2.2

**The poverty line using income support/income-based jobseeker's allowance, January 2002**

**£ per week**

| | |
|---|---|
| Single person aged 18-24 | £42.00 |
| Single person aged 25+ | £53.05 |
| Couple (both aged 18+) | £83.25 |
| Couple (both 18+ but under 60) with three children aged under 11 | £192.10 |
| Lone parent (aged 18+) with one child under 11 | £100.50 |
| Single pensioner (aged 60-74) | £92.15 |
| Pensioner couple (aged 60-74) | £140.55 |

Source: Department for Work and Pensions, Analytical Services Division, Information Centre, 20 February 2002

## Government poverty indicators

The UK government and the Scottish Executive publish annual reports on a series of poverty indicators. These are grouped under five broad subjects – children, young people, people of working age, older people and communities – each with its own set of targets. Some of these indicators are used in this chapter. Critics note that 'there is a lack of clarity about what this combination of indicators tells us'.[9] Further, government indicators are focused on policy objectives, and provide information on progress in that area; they are also subject to change as government priorities change.[10] The abundance of indicators creates a temptation for governments to highlight only successful results.

The Government is now considering and consulting on the creation of a new child poverty measure. Four options are being examined:[11]

- using a small number of indicators (for example, education and unemployment) to track low income;
- constructing an index using specified indicators to produce an overall figure;
- producing an overall figure that combines relative low income and material deprivation;
- using a core set of indicators of low income and consistent poverty.

## How many people live in poverty?

Different measures of poverty have their own advantages and disadvantages. The tables that follow cover data on HBAI and income support and key benefits.

## Households Below Average Income

HBAI gives a picture of the number of people living on low incomes in Britain as a whole. The figures include people receiving benefits and those working, but do not cover those who are homeless or who are living in residential institutions such as hostels or hospitals. Some Scottish data is also available, although figures do not include those people living north of the Caledonian Canal.

Table 2.3

**Percentage of individuals in households with below both 50 per cent mean income, and 60 per cent median income (after housing costs and including self-employed), 1979-2000/01, UK**

| Year | 50% mean | | 60% median | |
| --- | --- | --- | --- | --- |
| | Percentage | Number (millions) | Percentage | Number (millions) |
| 1979 | 9 | 5.0 | 13 | 7.1 |
| 1981 | 11 | 6.2 | 15 | 8.1 |
| 1987 | 19 | 10.5 | 20 | 11.1 |
| 1988/98 | 22 | 12.0 | 23 | 12.6 |
| 1990/91 | 24 | 13.5 | 24 | 13.5 |
| 1991/92 | 25 | 13.9 | 25 | 13.9 |
| 1992/93 | 25 | 14.1 | 24 | 13.9 |
| 1993/94 | 24 | 13.7 | 24 | 13.5 |
| 1994/95 | 24 | 13.4 | 23 | 13.4 |
| 1995/96 | 24 | 14.1 | 25 | 14.2 |
| 1996/97 | 25 | 14.1 | 25 | 13.9 |
| 1997/98 | 25 | 14.0 | 24 | 13.5 |
| 1998/99 | 25 | 14.3 | 24 | 13.4 |
| 1999/00 | 25 | 14.0 | 23 | 13.3 |
| 2000/01 | 24 | 13.7 | 23 | 12.9 |

Source: Department for Work and Pensions, *Households Below Average Income 2000/01*, 2002, Tables H1 and 3.3

Note: Figures from 1979 to 1995/96 are from the *Family Expenditure Survey*. Figures from 1996/97 onwards are from the *Family Resources Survey*.

Table 2.3 gives both the number and percentage of the general population living on incomes of below 50 per cent mean and 60 per cent median earnings since 1979. Figure 2.1 shows the number of households below the 60 per cent median income threshold, from 1979 to 2000/01.

Table 2.3 shows that since 1979, the proportion of people living in poverty (below 50 per cent mean income) has increased from 9 per cent of the population (5.0 million people) to 24 per cent of the population (13.7 million people) in 2001. If the 60 per cent median income line is followed over the same period, Figure 2.1 shows that the proportion of those living on low income grew from 13 per cent of the population (7.1 million) to 23 per cent of the population (12.9 million people).

Figure 2.1

**The number of households below 60 per cent median income (after housing costs and including self-employed) 1979-2000/01, UK**

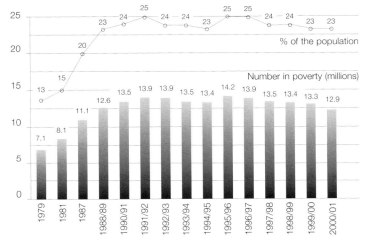

Source: Department for Work and Pensions, *Households Below Average Income 2000/01*, 2002, Tables H1 and 3.3

After a steep rise in the 1980s, there was a reduction in the 1990s in the rate of growth of poverty in the UK. But the number of people in poverty remains at a disturbingly high level.

Table 2.4 shows the percentage of individuals living below the thresholds in Scotland in 2000/01.

In Scotland in 2000/01, around a quarter of individuals lived in low-income households: 25 per cent below the 50 per cent average and 24 per cent below the 60 per cent median threshold. This is slightly higher than the Great Britain average.

## Children

Over the last thirty years there has been a steady growth in child poverty. According to government sources, children are over-represented at the bottom of the income distribution and under-represented at the top:

Table 2.4

**Percentage of individuals living in households below 50 per cent mean and 60 per cent median thresholds (after housing costs and including self employed), 2000/01, GB, Scotland, England and Wales**

|  | Below 50% mean | Below 60% median |
|---|---|---|
| Scotland | 25 | 24 |
| England | 24 | 22 |
| Wales | 26 | 24 |
| Great Britain | 24 | 23 |

Source: Department for Work and Pensions, *Households Below Average Income 2000/01*, 2002, Tables 3.6 and 4.6

> 'Children are now the group most likely to be in low-income households, and most likely to remain in low-income households for a long period of time.'[12]

The impact of poverty is wide ranging, and this has implications for both the quality of life and the life chances of those it affects. This is particularly true for children. Children born or brought up in poverty often go without essentials. According to the Child Poverty Action Group, 2.4 million children in the UK lack basic necessities such as a warm home and three adequate meals a day. For many, poverty also means living without access to the services and social activities that the majority of children take for granted.[13]

Table 2.5 shows the percentage of children in the UK living in households with incomes below both thresholds, from 1979 to 2001.

In 2000/01 around a third of children (32 per cent) in the UK lived in households with incomes below the 50 per cent average, and 31 per cent below the 60 per cent median threshold. Around one in three children live in poverty in the UK. In recent years there has been a slow fall in the number of children living in poverty.

Table 2.6 shows the percentage of children below the thresholds in Great Britain, Scotland, England and Wales in 2000/01.

In Scotland in 2000/01 around a third (32 per cent) of children lived in households with incomes below the 50 per cent average threshold and 30 per cent below the 60 per cent median threshold. There has been a slight increase in child poverty in Scotland between 1999/00 and

Table 2.5

**Percentage of children living in households with below 50 per cent mean, and 60 per cent median income (after housing costs and including self-employed), 1979-2000/01, UK**

| Year | Below 50% average | Below 60% median |
|------|------------------|------------------|
| 1979 | 10 | 14 |
| 1981 | 16 | 20 |
| 1987 | 24 | 25 |
| 1988/89 | 25 | 26 |
| 1990/91 | 31 | 31 |
| 1991/92 | 32 | 32 |
| 1992/93 | 33 | 33 |
| 1993/94 | 32 | 32 |
| 1994/95 | 32 | 32 |
| 1995/96 | 34 | 35 |
| 1996/97 | 35 | 34 |
| 1997/98 | 34 | 33 |
| 1998/99 | 35 | 33 |
| 1999/00 | 34 | 32 |
| 2000/01 | 32 | 31 |

Source: Department for Work and Pensions, *Households Below Average Income 2000/01*, 2002, Table H2

Note: Figures for 1979 to 1995/96 are from the *Family Expenditure Survey*. Figures from 1996/97 onwards are from the *Family Resources Survey*.

Table 2.6

**Percentage of children living in households with incomes below 50 per cent mean, and 60 per cent median thresholds (after housing costs and including self-employed), 2000/01, GB, Scotland, England and Wales**

| | Below 50% mean | Below 60% median |
|------|------------------|------------------|
| Scotland | 32 | 30 |
| England | 32 | 30 |
| Wales | 35 | 33 |
| Great Britain | 32 | 31 |

Source: Department for Work and Pensions, *Households Below Average Income 2000/01*, 2002

Figure 2.2

**Proportions of children and individuals living in low-income households (below 60 per cent median income, after housing costs, including self-employed), 1979-2000/01, UK**

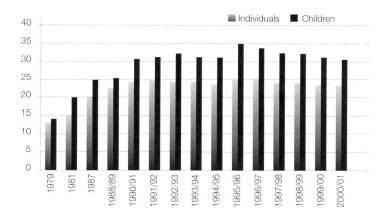

Source: Department for Work and Pensions, *Households Below Average Income 2000/01*, 2002, Tables H1 and 3.3

2000/01. In 1999/00, 29 per cent of children in Scotland lived in households with incomes below both thresholds.

Figure 2.2 shows the proportion of individuals and children in the UK living in households below 60 per cent median income, from 1979 to 2001.

While poverty has increased for the whole population since 1979, the rise in the proportion of children facing poverty has been worse. In 2000/01 around 3.9 million children in the UK lived in poverty.

The UK and Scottish governments' commitments to reduce poverty, particularly child poverty, has been made very clear. But, as the figures above show, child poverty remains at a disturbingly high level and the rate of change is relatively slow. The latest data showed that since 1997 in the UK, around half a million children were moved out of poverty; this is well below the Government's own estimate that around 1.2 million children would be lifted out of poverty in this period. The main beneficiaries have been children in households with incomes just below the poverty threshold.

Commentators note that the task now facing the Government is to lift children who are 'a long way below the threshold and every child some way above it'.[14]

## Family type

The likelihood of experiencing poverty is not spread evenly across society: some groups are much more vulnerable than others. A distinction should also be made between the proportion of all people in poverty who come from a particular group and the proportion within that group who experience poverty. So, for example, while lone parents make up a relatively small proportion of the total of people in poverty, a very high proportion of people who are lone parents are poor. Table 2.7 shows the overall distribution of poverty among family types.

Lone parent and single pensioner households, continue to be over-represented among those in poverty. It is worth noting that since 1995/96, households of couples with children form a decreasing proportion of those in poverty while lone-parent households form an increasing proportion.

Table 2.7

**Proportion of various household types in population and among low-income households (after housing costs and including self-employed), 2000/01, UK**

| Family type | % of total population | % below 50% mean income income | % below 60% median income |
|---|---|---|---|
| Pensioner couple | 9 | 9 | 9 |
| Single pensioner | 7 | 10 | 9 |
| Couple with children | 35 | 32 | 33 |
| Couple without children | 21 | 11 | 11 |
| Single with children | 9 | 20 | 20 |
| Single without children | 18 | 17 | 17 |
| All | 100 | 100 | 100 |
| All (millions) | 56.9 | 13.7 | 12.9 |

Source: Department for Work and Pensions, *Households Below Average Income 2000/01*, 2002, Table 3.3

Figure 2.3

**Over/under-representation of family types in low-income households (below 60 per cent median income), 2000/01, UK**

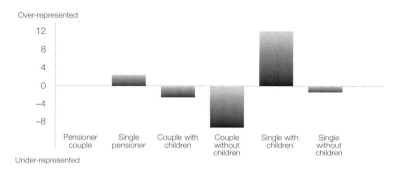

Source: Department for Work and Pensions, *Households Below Average Income 2000/01*, 2002, Table 3.3

Note: Over/under-representation is the difference between the proportion of a family type in the population as a whole, and the proportion of that family type among low-income households.

Figure 2.3 shows the over and under-representation of various household types among low-income households.

Table 2.8 and Figure 2.4 show the percentage within each family type facing poverty.

There was a sharp rise, in 1998/99, in the percentage of low-income, single pensioner and lone-parent households in the UK. In 2000/01 there has been a reduction, but the proportion of these households in poverty is still very high.

Between a third and quarter of single pensioners live in households below the thresholds.

Over half of lone-parent families live in poverty. Lone parents are over twice as likely as couples with children, and over four times as likely as couples without children, to be poor.

Table 2.8 shows that there has been a slight increase, between 1998/99 and 2000/01, in the proportion of low-income households of couples without children, and a slow reduction in the proportion of couples with children.

Table 2.8

**Proportion of each family type living in low-income households (after housing costs and including self-employed), 1994/95, 1998/99, 2000/01, UK**

| | 1994/95 | | 1998/99 | | 2000/01 | |
| | 50% | 60% | 50% | 60% | 50% | 60% |
| Family type | mean | median | mean | median | mean | median |
|---|---|---|---|---|---|---|
| Pensioner couple | 23 | 23 | (25) | 23 | (24) | (22) |
| Single pensioner | (32) | (31) | (37) | (33) | (32) | (28) |
| Couple with children | (23) | (23) | (24) | (22) | 22 | 21 |
| Couple without children | 12 | 12 | 12 | 11 | 13 | 12 |
| Single with children | (55) | (55) | (62) | (59) | (56) | (54) |
| Single without children | 23 | 23 | 22 | 22 | 23 | (22) |
| | | | | | | |
| All family types (%) | 24 | 24 | 25 | 24 | 24 | 23 |
| All family types (millions) | 13.3 | 13.1 | 14.3 | 13.4 | 13.7 | 12.9 |

Source: Department for Work and Pensions, *Households Below Average Income 2000/01*, 2002, Tables F1 and J1

Note: Estimates in brackets () are particularly uncertain.

Figure 2.4

**Risk of poverty by family type (60 per cent median, after housing costs, including self-employed), 2000/01, UK**

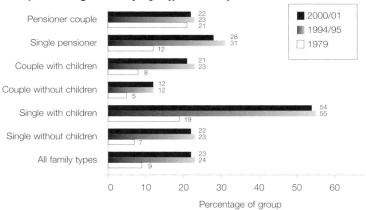

Source: Department for Work and Pensions, *Households Below Average Income 2000/01*, 2002, Tables F1 and J1

# Scotland

Data on average income and sources of income are also available for Scotland. Tables 2.9 and 2.10 show average weekly household income and income source in Scotland, compared with the UK and other regions. Note that there are marked differences in income levels within Scotland, as well as between Scotland and the UK as a whole.

The pattern of income by source varies across the UK. In Scotland, a larger percentage of average income comes from wages and social security benefits compared to the UK. Scotland has a lower than average income sourced in investments or income from self-employment.

In 1999/2000 the average income in Scotland was £336, which was lower than the Great Britain average of £349.

In Scotland, couples with and without children and single households without children had the highest weekly incomes. The weekly income of couples with children in Scotland (£360) was higher than the average for similar households (£345) in Great Britain.

Scottish single households with children have the lowest incomes at £204 a week. This is below the Great Britain average (£216) for the same family type.

## Income support

Tables 2.11 and 2.12 show the numbers of income support claimants and recipients in Scotland. With all means-tested benefits, individuals may

Table 2.9

**Percentage of gross weekly household income by source, 1997/98-1999/2000, UK**

|  | England | Wales | Scotland | N.Ireland | UK |
|---|---|---|---|---|---|
| Wage/salaries | 67 | 61 | 68 | 63 | 67 |
| Self-employment | 9 | 7 | 6 | 9 | 8 |
| Investment | 5 | 4 | 3 | 2 | 4 |
| Annuities/pensions | 7 | 8 | 7 | 4 | 7 |
| Social security benefits | 12 | 19 | 15 | 21 | 12 |
| Other sources | 1 | 2 | 1 | 1 | 1 |

Source: Down, *Family Spending*, Report on the 1999-2000 *Family Expenditure Survey*, 2002

Table 2.10

**Mean equivalised net weekly income by family type (before housing costs),1999/2000, Scotland and GB**

|  | Scotland | % of income for Scotland | GB | % of income for GB |
|---|---|---|---|---|
| Pensioner couple | 283 | 84.2 | 296 | 84.8 |
| Single pensioner | 277 | 82.4 | 267 | 76.5 |
| Couple with children | 360 | 107.1 | 345 | 98.9 |
| Couple without children | 397 | 118.2 | 443 | 126.9 |
| Single with children | 204 | 60.7 | 216 | 61.9 |
| Single without children | 333 | 99.1 | 371 | 106.3 |
| All | 336 | 100.0 | 349 | 100.0 |

Source: Scottish Executive, *Social Justice Annual Report: indicators of progress*, 2001, Table 1

claim both on their own behalf and for their dependants. So, although the statistics count only claimants, there may be other members of the household dependent on the benefit. It is important to determine the number of partners and dependants of claimants in order to give a better estimate of the numbers in poverty. It should be noted that dependency ratios vary for different client groups. Lone parents, for example, are more likely to have dependants than pensioners.

The total number of people in Scotland living on income support in November 2001 was 668,000. This includes claimants, their partners and dependants. The percentage of the Scottish population receiving income support (13.1 per cent) was above the Great Britain average of 11.7 per cent.

It should be noted that the numbers of income support claimants in Scotland fell from 409,000 in 1997 to 399,000 in 1999, although since 2000 there has been a rise in the number of claimants. In 2001 there were 421,000 income support claimants in Scotland, which is higher than in 1997. The reasons for the rise in numbers of claimants are not clear.[15]

Table 2.12 shows both the proportion of different claimant groups claiming income support and the percentage each forms of the population aged 16 and over, in Scotland and Great Britain.

There is a higher proportion of the Scottish population aged 16 and over (10.2 per cent) that claims income support compared with the Great Britain average of 8.5 per cent.

Table 2.11

**Income support recipients, November 2001, thousands and percentages, Scotland and GB**

| | Scotland | | GB | |
|---|---|---|---|---|
| | **Number (thousands)** | **% of Scottish population** | **Number (thousands)** | **% of GB population** |
| Claimants | 421 | 8.3 | 3950 | 6.8 |
| Partners | 54 | 1.1 | 574 | 1.0 |
| Dependants | 193 | 3.8 | 2247 | 3.9 |
| Totals | 668 | 13.1 | 6770 | 11.7 |

Source: Department for Work and Pensions, *Income Support Quarterly Statistical Enquiry, November 2001*, 2001

Table 2.12

**Income support claimants by claimant group, November 2001, Scotland and GB**

| | Scotland | | GB | |
|---|---|---|---|---|
| | **Claimants** | **% of Scottish population aged 16+** | **Claimants** | **% of GB population aged 16+** |
| All claimants (=100%) | 421,000 | 10.2 | 3,950,000 | 8.5 |
| Aged 60 or over (%) | 43.2 | 4.4 | 44.1 | 3.7 |
| Lone parents (%) | 18.8 | 1.9 | 22.0 | 1.9 |
| Disabled (%) | 30.0 | 3.1 | 26.4 | 2.2 |
| Other (%) | 8.1 | 0.8 | 7.5 | 0.6 |

Source: Department for Work and Pensions, *Income Support Quarterly Statistical Enquiry*, November 2001, 2001

Those aged 60 and over and disabled people, make up the largest claimant groups. Among income support claimants there is a bigger proportion of disabled claimants in Scotland (30 per cent) than Great Britain (26.4 per cent).

## Key benefits

As families claiming other benefits may only be marginally better off than those living on income support, which is itself a very meagre poverty line, we include some information on the numbers of people claiming other benefits.

Table 2.13 shows the percentage of households receiving various benefits, including income support, in 1999/2000. There is a higher proportion of households in Scotland receiving housing and council tax benefits than in Great Britain as a whole. Both of these benefits are means-tested and are administered by the local authority. Housing benefit can be claimed by anyone who is liable to pay rent and whose income falls below a prescribed level, and it is therefore available both to people

Table 2.13

**Percentage of households (column percentages) receiving various benefits, 1999/2000, Scotland, England, Wales and GB**

|  | Scotland | England | Wales | GB |
|---|---|---|---|---|
| Family credit/working families' tax credit | 3 | 3 | 3 | 3 |
| Income support | 15 | 12 | 14 | 13 |
| Housing benefit | 24 | 17 | 18 | 18 |
| Council tax benefit | 29 | 22 | 24 | 22 |
| Retirement pension | 29 | 30 | 33 | 30 |
| Jobseeker's allowance | 5 | 5 | 4 | 4 |
| Incapacity benefit | 9 | 5 | 10 | 6 |
| Attendance allowance | 4 | 3 | 5 | 3 |
| Invalid care allowance | 2 | 1 | 2 | 2 |
| Disability living allowance | 13 | 10 | 19 | 11 |
| Child benefit | 27 | 29 | 29 | 29 |
| On any income-related benefit | 34 | 26 | 30 | 27 |
| On any non-income-related benefit | 66 | 65 | 71 | 66 |
| On any benefit | 72 | 69 | 76 | 70 |
| No benefits | 28 | 31 | 24 | 30 |
| **Total households (base=100%)** | **2,183** | **21,447** | **1,358** | **24,988** |

Source: Department of Social Security, *Family Resources Survey Great Britain 1999-2000*, 2001, Table 3.10

receiving social security benefits and to those who are in employment. Council tax benefit can be claimed by anyone who is liable to pay council tax on the accommodation which is normally her/his home and who has sufficiently low income.

In 1999/2000 around a third of Scottish households (34 per cent) claimed income-related benefits, in contrast to just over a quarter of Great Britain households (27 per cent). Scotland has the highest percentage of households claiming income related benefits.

Households in Scotland receive the highest percentage of housing and council tax benefit. This may be a consequence of the higher proportion of people in public sector housing. In May 2001 there were 447,000 recipients of housing benefit and 528,000 recipients of council tax benefit in Scotland.[16]

Scotland has a lower proportion of households receiving retirement pensions and child benefit.

Table 2.14 shows the proportion of male and female claimants of key benefits by client group for Scotland and Great Britain in August 2001.

In August 2001 in Scotland, 18 per cent of people of working age claimed key benefits. This compares with the Great Britain average of 14 per cent. There were slightly more men of working age (18 per cent) than women (17 per cent).

The largest client group comprised sick and disabled claimants. Scotland has a higher percentage of claimants from this client group (11 per cent) than the Great Britain average (8 per cent).

Figure 2.5 below shows the percentage of claimants of key benefits between 1995 and 2001 in Scotland and the UK.

Table 2.14

**Claimants of key benefits[1] by client group and by gender, August 2001, Scotland and GB**

|  | Scotland | | GB | |
|---|---|---|---|---|
|  | **1,000s** | **% of working age[2]** | **1,000s** | **% of working age[2]** |
| **Unemployed** | 107 | 3 | 895 | 2 |
| males | 81 | 5 | 670 | 4 |
| females | 26 | 2 | 225 | 1 |
| **Sick/disabled** | 356 | 11 | 2,991 | 8 |
| males | 202 | 12 | 1,742 | 9 |
| females | 154 | 10 | 1,249 | 7 |
| **Lone parents** | 79 | 2 | 871 | 2 |
| males | 4 | 0 | 44 | 0 |
| females | 75 | 5 | 827 | 5 |
| **Others[3]** | 21 | 1 | 203 | 1 |
| males | 15 | 1 | 148 | 1 |
| females | 6 | 0 | 56 | 0 |
| **All** | 563 | 18 | 4,961 | 14 |
| males | 302 | 18 | 2,603 | 14 |
| females | 261 | 17 | 2,358 | 14 |

Source: Department for Work and Pensions Information Centre, 20 March 2002

Notes:

1 'Key benefits' are jobseekers's allowance, incapacity benefit, severe disability allowance, disability living allowance and income support.

2 Denominator for male and female percentages is all males/females of working age.

3 'Others' category includes income support claimants not included in the other groups – eg, carers, asylum seekers, pensioners (minimum income guarantee).

In 1995, 21 per cent of the working-age population claimed at least one key benefit. By August 2001 the proportions had fallen to 18 per cent. The decrease reflects increased employment, and various benefit changes. However, there has been little reduction in the percentage of people of working age claiming key benefits since 1999.

Figure 2.5

**Percentage[1] of claimants of key benefits,[2] August 1995 to August 2001, Scotland and GB**

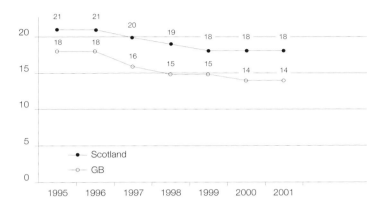

Source: Department for Work and Pensions Information Centre, 20 March 2002

Notes:
1 Percentage of working-age population of Scotland and GB respectively.
2 'Key benefits' are jobseekers's allowance, incapacity benefit, severe disability allowance, disability living allowance and income support.

## Notes

1   C Oppenheim, *Poverty: the facts*, Child Poverty Action Group, 1993

2   C Oppenheim and L Harker, *Poverty: the facts*, Child Poverty Action Group, 1996

3   Social Exclusion Unit leaflet, Cabinet Office, July 2000

4   The Commission on Social Justice, *The Justice Gap*, IPPR, 1993

5   J Roll, *Understanding Poverty: a guide to the concepts and measures*, Family Policy Studies Centre, 1992

6   See note 5

7   See note 2

8   A Sinfield, *Tackling and Preventing Poverty*, Memorandum to Scottish Affairs Committee, March 2000

9   W Paxton, 'Defining Moment', *New Start*, Vol 4, No 139, January 2002

10  G Palmer, 'Developing Poverty Indicators', *Poverty Today*, June/July 2001

11 Department for Work and Pensions, *Measuring Child Poverty: a consultation document*, 2002

12 Department for Work and Pensions, *Households Below Average Incomes, 1999/2000*, 2001

13 *Campaigns Extra*, Child Poverty Action Group, August 2001

14 J Bradshaw, 'Child Poverty under Labour', in G Fimister (ed), *An End in Sight? Tackling child poverty in the UK,* Child Poverty Action Group, 2001

15 Information Centre, Analytical Services Division, *Income Support Quarterly Statistical Enquiry*, Department for Work and Pensions, November 2001

16 Analytical Services Division, Work and Pension Statistics, Department for Work and Pensions, 2001

# Three
# Factors leading to poverty

The factors which cause and sustain poverty are complex, inter-linked and not easily identifiable. For example, fluctuations in global markets may cause a loss of local jobs but the connection may not be immediately apparent. Furthermore, it is not always a straightforward matter to separate the causes of poverty from its effects. This section looks at some of these factors linked to poverty.

## Industrial and economic change

New technologies have brought about radical structural changes in economies and industries. Easier movement of goods, services and money facilitated the growth of global markets, intensified competitiveness and has forced restructuring in local and national industries.

Scotland has a small domestic market and it is very dependent on exports and inward investment. It is therefore vulnerable to changes in global economic trends. For example, in recent times many electronics jobs were lost as the printed circuit board industry restructured to adapt to international competition. Large-scale job losses such as these have severe consequences for local economies.[1] Like the rest of the UK, Scotland has also witnessed a decline in its industrial and manufacturing base and a rise in employment in the 'service' sector. There has been a growth in part-time, flexible and short-term work patterns. While these changes do have some advantages, for many workers they result in low wages, fewer employment rights and insecurity of employment.

Figure 3.1 shows changes in the distribution of employment in Scotland by industrial sector between 1990 and 2000. After rapid growth in the 1980s, the number of people in Scotland employed in the service sector has continued to increase, albeit at a slower rate. The main growth areas in the service sector have been: distribution, hotel and catering, the finance sector, public administration and related services. The number of people working in manufacturing continues to decline. For example,

Figure 3.1

**Changes in the distribution of employment in Scotland by industrial sector, June 1990, June 1995 and June 2000**

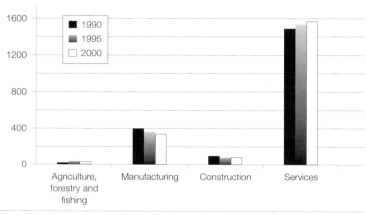

Source: Scottish Executive, *Scottish Economic Statistics 2001*, 2001

between January 2001 and February 2002 around 18,000 manufacturing jobs were lost in Scotland.[2] It should be noted that there are geographical and intra-sectoral variations.

## Changing households

There have been significant demographic changes over the last twenty years, which are reflected in the altered shape of households in which we live. Among the most significant changes are: an ageing population; a decrease in family size; a decline in the number of couples who marry; more children (around a third) born outside marriage, the majority to cohabiting couples; an increased divorce rate and a growth in the numbers of lone-parent households: 'Some family forms reflect changing social and economic trends; others have always existed, but have become more visible.'[3]

Projections over the next twenty-five years suggest that the population of Scotland will fall. There will be a steady increase in the number of people of pensionable age, and a decrease in the number of children

Table 3.1

## Projected population of Scotland (2000-based), by age group, 2000-2025

| Age group | 2000 (base) | 2001 | 2006 | 2011 | 2016 | 2021 | 2025 |
|---|---|---|---|---|---|---|---|
| All ages | 5,115 | 5,109 | 5,078 | 5,047 | 5,014 | 4,973 | 4,926 |
| Children under 16 | 1,001 | 988 | 917 | 845 | 807 | 796 | 784 |
| Working ages | 3,190 | 3,194 | 3,209 | 3,208 | 3,220 | 3,183 | 3,076 |
| Pensionable ages | 924 | 927 | 951 | 993 | 987 | 994 | 1,066 |

Source: General Register Office for Scotland, 2001

Note: Pensionable age is 65 for men, 60 for women until 2010; between 2010 and 2020 pensionable age for women increases to 65.

Table 3.2

## Household type, Scotland, 1996 and 1999/2000

| | 1996 | 1999/2000 |
|---|---|---|
| Single adult | 13 | 15 |
| Small adult | 18 | 17 |
| Single parent | 5 | 6 |
| Small family | 17 | 15 |
| Large family | 9 | 8 |
| Large adult | 12 | 10 |
| Older smaller | 12 | 14 |
| Single pensioner | 14 | 16 |
| Total households | 100 | 100 |
| Base | | 30,227 |

Source: *Scottish House Condition Survey 1996*, Scottish Homes, Edinburgh; and Scottish Executive, *Scotland's People*, Results from the 1999/2000 *Scottish Household Survey*, Vol 3, 2001

Note: Single adult = 1 adult of non-pensionable age and no children; small adult = 2 adults of non-pensionable age and no children; single parent = 1 adult of any age and 1 or more children; small family = 2 adults and 1 or 2 children; large family = 2 adults and 3 or more children; older smaller = 1 adult of non-pensionable age and 1 of pensionable age and no children, or 2 adults of pensionable age and no children; single pensioner = 1 adult of pensionable age and no children.
Note: Percentages for 1999/2000 are taken from the *Scottish Household Survey*, which is conducted on the basis of samples. Variations in percentages may be found depending on the base number.

under 16. After initial growth the working-age population will also decrease. It should be noted that these projections could well change.

In Scotland since 1996, single adult, single pensioner and older smaller households have increased in number. There has also been a small increase in lone-parent households and a decrease in all other household types.

## Composition of workforce

The composition of the workforce has changed substantially in the last twenty years, and patterns of working have been transformed. There are increasing numbers of women in the workforce. In 1959, 47 per cent of women were in employment; by 2000 this had risen to 70 per cent. There has also been a growth in part-time and flexible working. In the UK (Spring 2001) around a fifth of full-time employees and almost a quarter of part-time employees had some type of flexible working arrangement such as term-time contracts.

Table 3.3 shows the percentage of people in employment in Scotland, by status and gender, from 1997 to 2000, and in the UK for 2001. Again, it should be noted that differences exist within the UK and Scotland.

Of individuals in employment in Scotland (2000) and the UK (2001), around three-quarters were in full-time employment and around a quarter were in part-time employment.

Around two-thirds of those in full-time employment were men, a third were women. The majority of those in part-time employment were women.

Around 90 per cent of male workers worked full time. Female workers were split more evenly between those who did full-time work (55.5 per cent) and those who did part-time work (44.5).

Table 3.3

**People in employment by status and gender, Scotland 1997 to 2000 and UK 2001**

|  | Scotland | | | | UK |
| --- | --- | --- | --- | --- | --- |
|  | 1997 | 1998 | 1999 | 2000 | 2001 |
| **All in employment (000s)** | 2,284 | 2,309 | 2,297 | 2,331 | 2,375 |
| full-time (%) | 76.2 | 75.7 | 74.7 | 74.6 | (75.1) |
| part-time (%) | 23.8 | 24.3 | 25.2 | 25.3 | (24.9) |
| males (%) | 53.9 | 53.9 | 53.5 | 53.8 | 53.3 |
| females (%) | 46.1 | 46.2 | 46.4 | 46.2 | 46.7 |
| **All full-time workers** | | | | | |
| males (%) | 64.9 | 64.8 | 64.9 | 65.6 | (66.7) |
| females (%) | 35.0 | 35.1 | 35.1 | 34.4 | (33.3) |
| **All part-time workers** | | | | | |
| males (%) | 18.4 | 19.4 | 19.7 | 18.8 | (20.1) |
| females (%) | 81.4 | 80.6 | 80.3 | 81.2 | (79.9) |
| **All male workers** | | | | | |
| full-time (%) | 91.8 | 91.2 | 90.7 | 91.1 | (90.9) |
| part-time (%) | 8.1 | 8.8 | 9.3 | 8.9 | (9.1) |
| **All female workers** | | | | | |
| full-time (%) | 57.9 | 57.6 | 56.6 | 55.5 | (55.7) |
| part-time (%) | 42.0 | 42.4 | 43.5 | 44.5 | (44.3) |

Source: Scottish Executive, Scottish Economic Statistics 2001, 2001

Note: Figures in brackets represent UK percentages and were obtained from National Statistics, *Labour Market Trends March 2002*, 2002

# Unemployment

The number of unemployed people in Britain increased substantially in the 1980s and 1990s, fuelled by major recessions in 1980-82 and 1990-92. Despite significant reductions in the rate of unemployment, large-scale unemployment remains a fact of life for many communities and thousands of families in Scotland.

Unemployment is not evenly spread; certain occupations, groups, individuals and geographical areas experience higher rates of unemployment. For example, semi-skilled or unskilled workers are four times more likely to be unemployed than professional/managerial workers.[6] Those most at risk of unemployment include unskilled and poorly qualified individuals, young people, people with disabilities, those in poor health, ethnic minorities, long-term unemployed and older men. Furthermore, European Union figures show that, on average, a child living in a household where there is no adult in paid work is four times more likely to grow up in poverty than a child living in a household with one adult working.[7]

Two main approaches are used to quantify unemployment in Britain: the claimant count and the International Labour Organisation (ILO) measure.

Table 3.4

**Employment[1], ILO unemployment[1] and claimant counts[2], 2002, Scotland, England, Wales, N. Ireland and UK**

|  | Scotland | England | Wales | N. Ireland | UK |
|---|---|---|---|---|---|
| All aged 16 and over (000s) | 4,051 | 39,636 | 2,329 | 1,284 | 47,300 |
| In employment (000s) | 2,372 | 24,081 | 1,253 | 715 | 23,420 |
| Employment rate[3] (%) | 72.9 | 75.3 | 68.5 | 67.2 | 74.5 |
| ILO unemployed (000s) | 170 | 1,246 | 75 | 46 | 1,538 |
| ILO unemployment rate[4] (%) | 6.7 | 4.9 | 5.7 | 6.1 | 5.1 |
| Total economic active (000s) | 2,541 | 25,327 | 1,329 | 761 | 29,958 |
| Economic activity rate[3] (%) | 78.2 | 79.3 | 72.7 | 71.7 | 78.6 |
| Claimant count (000s) | 104.3 | 763.7 | 47.5 | 37.6 | 953.0 |
| Rate[5] (%) | 4.2 | 3.0 | 3.7 | 4.8 | 3.2 |
| Economically inactive (000s) | 1,510 | 14,309 | 1000 | 523 | 17,342 |
| % of all aged 16 and over | 37.3 | 36.1 | 42.9 | 40.7 | 36.7 |

Source: *Labour Market Trends*, May 2002

Notes:
1 Figures for employment and ILO counts relate to period January-March 2002, seasonally adjusted.
2 Figures for claimant counts relate to April 2002.
3 Rate as a percentage of all people of working age.
4 Rate as a percentage of total economically active.
5 Rate as a percentage of the estimated total workforce.

The *claimant count* is the number of people registered each month as available for work at a job centre and claiming contribution-based job-seeker's allowance, income-based jobseeker's allowance or national insurance credits. The main disadvantage of this measure arises from its links with the benefit system: changes to benefits may affect the level of the count, as people who are not eligible for benefits may not bother to register. This results in the claimant count underestimating the number of those unemployed.

The *ILO definition* counts as unemployed those who (a) have not undertaken any work for pay or profit in the particular reference week; (b) want to work; (c) are available to start work within two weeks, and (d) have looked for work within the previous four weeks. This measure is inde-pendent of changes in the benefits system and is an internationally accepted standard. However, it does not allow analysis at local area level.

Figure 3.2

**Trends in ILO unemployment and claimant counts, 1992-2001, Scotland and UK**

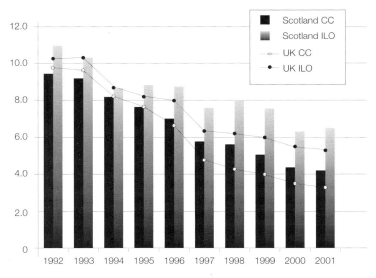

Source: National Statistics, StatBase – TimeZone – accessed online at www.statistics.gov.uk/statbase/timezone.asp

In April 2002 the claimant count for Scotland was 4.2 per cent, compared with 3.2 per cent for the UK. The ILO unemployment rate for Scotland was 6.7, compared with 5.1 for the UK. Unemployment was highest in Scotland. Economic inactivity was highest in Wales.

Since 1992 there has been decline in the number of people unemployed both in the UK and in Scotland. Since 1997 unemployment has declined more sharply in the UK than in Scotland. The claimant count rates are lower than the ILO rates and show sharper and steadier decline in unemployment. ILO rates show a small increase in unemployment in Scotland in 2001.

## Economic inactivity

Economically inactive people are those who are neither in employment nor classed by ILO as unemployed. This group comprises individuals who want a job but have not sought work for four weeks, or cannot start work immediately, and those who do not want a job. The latter includes people who are retired, students, sick and disabled people and those who have family responsibilities. The group also includes 'discouraged workers', that is, people who may want to work but believe that there are no jobs available and so do not look for them. In 2001 (Spring), unemployment as a proportion of the working-age population in UK was around 3.8 per cent. In comparison, economic inactivity was around 22 per cent, unchanged since 1993.[8]

Economic inactivity rates for women have declined from 35 per cent in 1984 to 28 per cent in 2001, but have increased for men in this period from 12 per cent to 16 per cent. The majority of economically inactive women (72 per cent) had family responsibilities. Sickness and disability are the main reasons for male economic inactivity. Among 25-34-year-old economically inactive men, 43 per cent were long-term sick or disabled; the figure rises to 64 per cent for men aged 35-49.[9] There has been an increase in economic inactivity among young people but this is largely to do with an increase in those staying on in full-time education.

Economic inactivity is often described as 'hidden unemployment'. For example, in 2001 there were more than five times as many working-age people who were economically inactive as there were unemployed.[10] It is high among groups who are vulnerable in the labour market, such as older people, lone parents, people with disabilities and people with few qualifications. It is also higher in disadvantaged areas. For example, Tyne and Wear, West Central Scotland, Wales, Merseyside and Inner London all have much higher rates of economic inactivity than the South East, the South West, the rest of Scotland or Outer London. However, it should be noted that 'there is evidence to suggest that differences within regions may well be larger than differences between regions'.[11]

Table 3.5 shows economic activity and inactivity broken down by status and gender in Scotland, 2001.

Table 3.5

**Economic activity by status (column percentages), Spring 2001, Scotland**

|  | All persons | Males | Females |
|---|---|---|---|
| **Economically active (000s)**[1] | 2,468 | 1,353 | 1,115 |
| Permanent employees (%) | 78.2 | 73.9 | 83.4 |
| Temporary employees (%) | 6.2 | 5.4 | 7.2 |
| Self-employed (%) | 8.5 | 12.1 | 4.0 |
| On government supported training and employment programmes (%) | – | 0.8 | – |
| **Economically inactive (000s)**[2] | 696 | 284 | 412 |
| Looking after family/home (%) | 24.9 | 6.0 | 37.9 |
| Student (%) | 20.4 | 24.3 | 17.7 |
| Other (%) | 54.9 | 70.1 | 44.4 |

Source: National Statistics, *Labour Market Trends 2002*, Women in the Labour Market, Table B

Notes:
1 Sub-categories are percentages of all economically active.
2 Sub-categories are percentages of all economically inactive.

In 2001 in Scotland, the majority of those economically active (78.2 per cent) were permanent employees. There were proportionately more women than men in this category (83.4 per cent of women; 73.9 per cent of men). Temporary employees and those self-employed were much fewer. Proportionately more men were self-employed and more women in temporary employment.

Of those economically inactive, over half were in the 'other' category that includes sick, disabled and retired people. The majority of economically inactive men (70 per cent) were in this category. Around a quarter of economically inactive people (24.9 per cent) looked after family; over a third of economically inactive women undertook this work. Just over a fifth of economically inactive people were students; around a quarter (24.3 per cent) were men and 17.7 per cent were women.

## Tackling 'worklessness'

The Labour Government has introduced a number of initiatives to deal with unemployment and economic inactivity. These include job action teams, the Job Transitions Service for areas hit by large-scale redundancies and employment zones. There are 15 employment zones established in areas of persistently high employment in Great Britain. Glasgow is one of them.

A key policy is the New Deal programme, introduced in 1998. New Deal programmes are targeted at specific groups such as young people, long-term unemployed, lone parents, and people with disabilities. They aim to help unemployed people into work by increasing their employability, through the provision of advice, training, work experience and support. The programmes are compulsory for some benefit claimants such as young people, but voluntary for others, such as those with disabilities.

We have included New Deal figures in the relevant sections, where they have been available. From May 2002, statistics on the New Deal will be published quarterly and can be obtained from the Scottish Executive or Office for National Statistics.

Many elements of the New Deal have received praise: in particular, the personal support, education and training elements. However there are concerns. First, improving 'employability' by increasing skills and confidence is vital in finding a job, but it does not guarantee one. Job availability, the economic climate, discrimination and geographical location are all factors in gaining employment. Second, the current focus on *paid work* does result in undervaluing or ignoring *unpaid work* done by those taking on family responsibilities. Finally, there is the use of compulsion. Participants who do not take part or fail to comply with the requirements of the programme have benefits stopped for a specified period. Since March 2000 those who breach the rules twice have benefits stopped for six months. It has been described as 'the toughest benefit penalties ever faced by British unemployed people'.[12] There is little evidence that sanctions change behaviour or encourage people back to work; rather, they tend to increase hardship.

## Poverty and work

The figures below highlight divisions in the distribution of work and also show that those in work are less likely to face poverty. Unsurprisingly the risk of poverty is lower for 'work-rich' two-earner couples than for 'work-poor' no-earner couples or for couples where part-time work is the only experience.

Table 3.6 and Figure 3.3 show the percentage of individual in each economic group with incomes below the 60 per cent median threshold in 1994/95, 1998/99 and 2000/01 in Great Britain.

Table 3.6

**Percentage of individuals (row percentages) below 60 per cent median equivalised income by economic status (after housing costs and including self-employed), 1994/95, 1998/99, 2000/01, GB**

|  | 1994/95 | 1998/99 | 2000/01 |
|---|---|---|---|
| Self-employed | 26 | 23 | 25 |
| Single/couple in full-time employment | 2 | 3 | 4 |
| One full-time, one part-time | 3 | 5 | 5 |
| One full-time, one not working | 15 | 20 | 20 |
| One/more part-time | 28 | 33 | 29 |
| Head/spouse aged 60+ | 29 | 30 | 28 |
| Head/spouse unemployed | 72 | 77 | 77 |
| Other | 58 | 61 | 61 |
| All types (%) | 24 | 24 | 23 |
| All types (millions) | 13.1 | 13.4 | 12.9 |

Source: Department for Work and Pensions, *Households Below Average Income 2000/01*, 2002, Table J2

Within all groups, as defined by economic status, there has been very little change in the proportion of people in poverty between 1994 and 2001 in Great Britain.

Single people and couples who are both in full-time work, or where one works full time and one part time, continue to have low rates of poverty.

Households headed by unemployed people continue to face the greatest risk of poverty. Just over three-quarters of such families lived in

Figure 3.3

**Percentage of individuals below 60 per cent median equivalised income by economic status (after housing costs and including self-employed), 1994/95, 1998/99, 2000/01, GB**

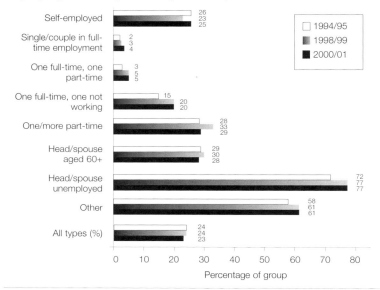

Source: Department for Work and Pensions, *Households Below Average Income 2000/01*, 2002, Table J2

poverty in 2000/01. There has been a slight growth in the group since 1994.

Around a quarter of self-employed people live in poverty. It is worth noting that a fifth of households where only one partner works full time, and 29 per cent of households where one or more person works part time, live in poverty. This suggests that entry into the labour market does not guarantee a route out of poverty.

The category 'other' includes the long-term sick, disabled people and non-working single parents. State benefits tend to be the main source of income for the majority of this group. Well over half of this group live in poverty. These figures show that benefits alone are not enough to lift people out of poverty.

## Second jobs and under-employment

Work patterns vary; they are influenced by factors such as availability of jobs, rates of pay, family commitments and personal choice. People with second jobs and those who are under-employed are examples of the variety of work patterns that exist.

In the UK since 1995, more than 1.2 million people had second jobs at each spring quarter. Part-time workers are almost three times more likely to have second jobs than full-time workers (7.9 per cent compared with 2.8 per cent respectively). It is worth noting that men with second jobs tend to earn more in their main job than men with one job. Women with second jobs earned less than those with one job. The differences were smaller for female part-time workers than full-time workers.[13]

Under-employment is defined as the mismatch between people's actual working patterns and their desired working patterns. Time-related under-employment is when a person wants to work longer hours than they do at present, either in their current job, a new job or an additional job. Table 3.7 shows the numbers and rate of time-related under-employment in Scotland and other regions. The 'rate' shown in the table represents the number of people who want to work longer as a proportion of all in employment.

Table 3.7

**Time-related under-employment, 2001, Wales, Scotland, England and N. Ireland**

|            | Thousands | Rate  |
| ---------- | --------- | ----- |
| Wales      | 123       | 9.9%  |
| Scotland   | 227       | 9.7%  |
| England    | 1990      | 8.5%  |
| N. Ireland | 32        | 4.8%  |

Source: Scottish Executive, *Scottish Economic Statistics 2001*, 2001

## Low pay

Employment is no guarantee of escaping poverty. The New Policy Institute notes that excluding pensioners 'almost half of both adults and children below the low-income threshold are in working households'.[14] Low pay is more prevalent in industries such as catering and hairdressing, and among such occupations such as cleaners, bar staff and checkout operators. Unskilled workers, women, ethnic minorities and young workers are all more likely than others to be low paid. Low-paid jobs tend to be more insecure: low-paid workers are 2.7 times more likely to be unemployed in the following year than those in high paid jobs.[15]

Many low-paid workers are dependent on in-work benefits to meet their needs, which means, in effect, that the state is supporting employers who pay low wages. Such workers cannot afford private pensions, or insurance policies for mortgage or unemployment protection. Many are not paid enough to be included in the national insurance scheme, with the result that they are not eligible for contributory benefits such as statutory sick pay or basic state retirement pension. The Low Pay Unit estimated that in 2000 around 2.5 million workers earned below the lower earning limit.[16]

In April 1999 the national minimum wage was introduced, covering all workers aged 22 or over. A lower rate was introduced for 18–21-year-olds.

'The national minimum wage sets the floor below which wages must not fall and prevents gross exploitation of workers who have least bargaining power.'[17]

Table 3.8

**Low pay definitions, 2002**

|  | £ per hour | £ per week |
|---|---|---|
| Low Pay Unit's threshold | £7.32 | £277.24 |
| Council of Europe's decency threshold | £7.97 | £302.12 |
| Half male median earnings | £5.38 | £203.85 |
| National minimum wage | £4.10 | £155.39 |

Source: Low Pay Unit, 2002

Note: Low Pay Unit's threshold is calculated using 2/3 male median earnings; Council of Europe's decency threshold is calculated using 68% average earnings; all calculations based on a working week of 37.9 hours.

Table 3.8 gives current rates of minimum wage and two other low pay benchmarks. In each case anything below the rate is regarded as low pay.

## Effects of minimum wage

Around 1.3 million workers were entitled to the minimum wage in March 2001. Around two-thirds were part-time workers and around 70 per cent were women. The Low Pay Unit estimates that between 1998 and April 2000 the gender pay gap was reduced by 2 per cent, and between April 1999 and April 2000 women's average part-time earnings increased by 2 per cent. Young people aged between 18 and 21 years also benefited. Between April 1998 and 1999, for example, the proportion of young hairdressers earning below £3 an hour fell from 10 per cent to 1 per cent. The increase in the national minimum wage levels in October 2002 to £4.10 is expected to benefit 120,000 workers (6.1 per cent) in Scotland.[18]

The majority of employers comply with minimum wage legislation, but there is a significant minority who do not. In Spring 2001, 320,000 people aged 18 or over in the UK were paid less than the minimum wage rates.[19] Some of these workers did not receive the rate for legitimate reasons (for example, if they were on accredited courses), but many did not receive the wages to which they were entitled. In 2000 it is estimated that around 170,000 workers entitled to a minimum wage did not receive it. While incidences of non-compliance are to be found in all sectors, they are highest in the services sector. Many workers are afraid to complain in case they lose their jobs.[20]

## Discrimination

There are strong links between discrimination, social exclusion and poverty. Discrimination is a major factor in the creation of social exclusion, as its effects can result in the denial of a range of rights, and in the most severe cases violence and loss of life. The relation between poverty and discrimination is more complex. While they are closely linked, discrimination does not automatically lead to poverty. Many people who face discrimination are not poor. However discrimination affects life chances by restricting access to the labour market, to services such as health, education and housing, and remains a root cause of much poverty.

## Personal circumstances

Personal circumstances also affect the risk of being poor. Having children, a long-term illness or a disability are not in themselves causes of poverty, but they all impose extra costs on families and individuals, and can limit access to employment. A combination of these factors often results in extreme vulnerability to poverty.

## Individual behaviour

A number of commentators have argued that, in various different ways, individual behaviour is the primary cause of poverty. Their arguments include the claims that poverty is caused by individual fecklessness; that poverty is cultural and is passed down through families; that there is an underclass which has become separated (or has separated itself) from society and for which poverty is a deliberately chosen condition; and that dependency on benefits weakens people's resolve to work, thus consigning them to poverty. However, while such arguments may carry some instinctive appeal to the unaffected onlooker, there is little evidence to substantiate them. Moreover, these claims do not allow the possibility of influence by other factors, and take no account of the large-scale structural forces that shape people's lives.

## Government policies

Government priorities and policies have considerable impact on the growth of poverty. Key areas are tax and benefit policies.

## Benefits

The cost of social security remains a major source of concern for governments. Social security spending has steadily increased since the founding of the welfare state. However, the proportion of national income spent on social security in the UK remains in the mid-range for European Union countries. Commentators point out that expenditure is directly related to structural factors such as recession, unemployment and the failures of related government policies. For example, improvements in the economic climate saw social security expenditure as a percentage of GDP (gross domestic product) fall from 13 per cent in 1993/94 to 11 per cent in 1998/99.[21]

The Labour Government has made tackling poverty and social exclusion a priority. In particular there is a clear commitment to end child poverty. A number of measures have been introduced to achieve these aims. These include: the working families' tax credit, a means-tested benefit introduced to help parents in work; a 26 per cent rise in child benefit in real terms since 1997 and a 45 per cent rise in means-tested payments for children; a disability income guarantee for severely disabled people under 60 on income support; and the minimum income guarantee for pensioners. Benefit changes are linked to measures such as the national minimum wage, increased childcare benefits, and the New Deal. The majority of current government initiatives are focused around employment, and are intended to 'make work pay'. Government policies have had some beneficial effect, particularly for children, but there are concerns that less is being done for those who cannot work, those for whom work is not available and those who do unpaid work.

One of the most significant changes in this field since 1979 is that people who rely on benefits have seen their incomes decline relative to incomes in society at large. This is a result of increases in benefits being tied to prices rather than to average incomes, which have risen faster than prices. In 2000, income support was 20 per cent of average earnings, compared to 30 per cent in 1983.[22]

Further, in recent years, governments have favoured the use of 'targeted' or means-tested benefits, arguing that that they are the most efficient way of helping those most in need. However, means-testing involves complicated and expensive administration; there is a relatively low take-up of such benefits; and means-tested benefits also create poverty traps. People may also be discouraged from saving, because savings are taken into account when benefits are calculated.

The Government hopes to deal with some of these problems through greater integration between the tax and benefit systems and the use of tax credits. The aim is to increase incentives to work, and create a system that is easier to both understand and administer. But experience of working families' tax credit suggests that the system may not remove the problems commonly associated with means-testing, in particular the often negative interaction with housing benefit. There are also concerns about whether the new system can be sufficiently responsive to job changes or life changes such as a marriage breakdown.

The 2000/01 *Family Resources Survey* found that over a third of children (38 per cent) below the poverty line did not receive either income support or working families' tax credit:

> 'Some 1.5 million children who are seen to be in poverty are in families that do not receive the benefits that are the Government's principal instrument for attacking child poverty. This puts almost two in every five poor children out of reach of increases in mean-tested benefits making the child poverty target significantly harder to reach.'[23]

This could also explain why the latest figures for child poverty were higher than those predicted by a number of different agencies.

Governments use the benefit system both to reward and punish, in order to achieve policy aims or behavioural change. There is increasing concern at this government's use of benefit sanctions. These include loss of benefits for non-compliance in the New Deal, and the proposals for withdrawal of housing benefit for 'unsocial behaviour' and loss of child benefit for truancy. The Government sees sanctions as a way of ensuring that individuals take on their due responsibilities, in return for benefits received from society. However, current measures are more likely to increase poverty and hardship for families with multiple problems who are unable to cope.

## Taxation

During the 1980s, government policies on taxation favoured better-off groups, with the top rate of tax being reduced from 83 per cent to 40 per cent. In the 1990s, governments did introduce measures to help lower paid groups. For example, the standard rate of tax was reduced and a low bottom rate introduced. The current government's direct tax measures have been of most benefit to the poorest groups, while a healthy economy has also meant that the richest have not lost out.[24]

However over the past three decades there has also been a shift from tax on income (direct taxation) to tax on expenditure (indirect taxation), with the result that the poorest groups pay proportionately more in tax. Indirect taxation is regressive because it has a disproportionately adverse effect on poorer groups. As shown in Table 3.9, in 2000/01 the poorest fifth of households paid 6 per cent more of their income in all taxes than the richest fifth – 41 per cent compared with 35 per cent. In addition, tax concessions tend to favour better off groups. In 1999/2000, tax relief on private and occupational pensions amounted to £12 billion.[25]

Table 3.9

**All taxes as a percentage of gross income, by household, UK, 2000/01**

|  | **Direct** | **Indirect** | **All taxes** |
|---|---|---|---|
| Bottom fifth | 11.6 | 29.5 | 41.2 |
| Top fifth | 23.4 | 12.1 | 35.5 |
| All | 20.5 | 16.4 | 37.0 |

Source: *Economic Trends*, No 582, May 2002

## Wages differentials

Wage differentials exist, not just between men and women, and manual and non-manual workers, but also within these groups as Figure 3.4 shows. The pay gap between top directors and employees has also continued to grow. A study by the TUC found that the median annual salary and bonus for the highest paid director in a company grew from £201,000 in 1994 to £416,073 in 2001: an increase of 107 per cent. Median average pay for employees in the same companies rose by just 31 per cent.[26] Furthermore, many of the most highly paid also receive many fringe benefits, which are often not taken into account when income is assessed. These include travel and medical insurance, share options and generous pension schemes.

Figure 3.4

**Weekly pay dispersions for full-time workers, April 2000, £ per week, Scotland**

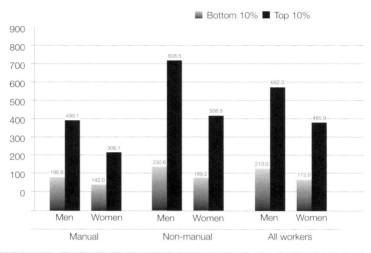

Source: *Scottish Economic Statistics 2001* (from Office for National Statistics, *New Earnings Survey*)

Note: The bottom 10% earns the amounts shown or less; the top 10% earn the amounts shown or more.

In Scotland in April 2000, weekly pay dispersions for full-time workers show that a gap of at least £450 per week existed between the lowest and highest paid men and of £300 between the highest and lowest paid women.

## Inequality

Inequalities in income and wealth in Britain remain higher than in most developed countries. During the 1980s these inequalities grew sharply; they appeared to stabilise in the 1990s but there are signs that they may once again be increasing.[27] Although there is a great deal of information available about poverty and the people who experience it, information on wealth and the wealthy is more difficult to obtain.

It should be noted that commentators distinguish between income and wealth. Income refers to money, which comes from salaries or state benefits. Wealth 'is about ownership of assets including money saved, property and investments'.[28] A distinction is also made between 'marketable wealth' (assets which owners can sell) and 'non-marketable wealth' (assets such as occupational pensions, which they cannot sell).

In the period between 1987 and 2000, wealth in the UK increased by an average of 4.6 per cent, adjusted for inflation.[29] In 1993 the wealth of the richest two hundred individuals in Britain was around £48.2 billion; in 2002 it had increased to £102 billion. The overall worth of the richest hundred individuals in Scotland rose from £7.7 billion in 2000 to £9.98 billion in 2001.[30]

Table 3.10 shows the share of marketable wealth for percentages of the population.

In 1999, in the UK, the richest 1 per cent owned almost a quarter (23 per cent) of the total marketable wealth. The wealthiest 10 per cent owned over half (54 per cent) of the total marketable wealth and the wealthiest 25 per cent owned around three-quarters of the total marketable wealth (74 per cent). The least wealthy half of the population owned only 6 per cent of marketable wealth between them.

Some people argue that inequalities do not matter as long as the overall standards of living are rising. In their view the task is to eradicate poverty and create equal opportunities for all. The issue however is more complex; relative poverty is determined by the norms and standards of a given society. General affluence raises the price of basic necessities and the costs of participating in that society, making it much more expensive

Table 3.10

**Distribution of marketable wealth, 1976 to 1999 (intermediate years), UK**

|  | 1976 | 1981 | 1986 | 1991 | 1996 | 1999 |
|---|---|---|---|---|---|---|
| Percentage of wealth owned by: | | | | | | |
| Most wealthy 1% | 21 | 18 | 18 | 17 | 20 | 23 |
| Most wealthy 5% | 38 | 36 | 36 | 35 | 40 | 43 |
| Most wealthy 10% | 50 | 50 | 50 | 47 | 50 | 54 |
| Most wealthy 25% | 71 | 73 | 73 | 71 | 74 | 74 |
| Most wealthy 50% | 92 | 92 | 90 | 92 | 93 | 94 |

Source: *Social Trends*, No 32, 2000, Table 5.24

for the poorest to afford these things, even with absolute improvements in living conditions. It is not possible to offer real equality of opportunity in deeply unequal societies.

'In a market economy affluence buys opportunities and opportunity becomes the new privilege.'[31]

Although, on average, standards of living have risen, the increasing affluence in the UK and in Scotland has not been shared equally by everyone. The poorest groups in society have seen little change, but the richest groups have benefited disproportionately. Table 3.11 shows the share of total income of the top and bottom 10 per cent income groups. Table 3.12 shows the change in the share of total income for these groups.

Table 3.11
**Share of total income by the top and bottom 10 per cent of the income distribution (after housing costs and including self-employed), 1994/95, 1996/97 and 2000/01, UK**

|  | 1994/95 | 1996/97 | 2000/01 |
|---|---|---|---|
| Bottom 10% of the income distribution | 2 | 2 | 2 |
| Top 10% of the income distribution | 27 | 28 | 29 |

Source: Department for Work and Pensions, *Households Below Average Income 2000/01*, 2002, Table A3

Table 3.12
**Change in share of total income by the top and bottom 10 per cent of the income distribution (after housing costs and including self-employed), 1994/95 to 2000/01, UK**

|  | % change from 1994/95 to 1999/00 |
|---|---|
| Bottom 10% of the income distribution | 0 |
| Top 10% of the income distribution | +7.4 |

Source: Department for Work and Pensions, *Households Below Average Income 2000/01*, 2002, Table A3

In the UK between 1994/5 and 2000/01, the share of total income for the poorest tenth of the population did not change from 2 per cent, while that of the richest tenth rose from 27 per cent to 29 per cent. During this period, this represents no change in the share of total income for the poorest tenth of the population, while the richest tenth saw its share rise by 7.4 per cent.

## Notes

1 R Tennant, *Globalisation and Poverty*, Briefing Sheet 11, Scottish Poverty Information Unit, April 2001
2 'Scottish Manufacturing Goes into Free Fall', Press Release, Labour Research Department, June 2002
3 *Gender Audit* 1997, Engender, 1997
4 *Social Trends*, No 32, Office for National Statistics, 2002
5 See note 4
6 M Howard, A Garnham, G Fimister and J Veit-Wilson, *Poverty: the facts*, Child Poverty Action Group, 2001
7 Innocenti Research Centre, *A League Table of Child Poverty in Rich Nations*, UNICEF, June 2000
8 C Barham, 'Economic Inactivity and the Labour Market', *Labour Market Trends*, Office for National Statistics, February 2002
9 See note 8
10 P Bivand, 'Economic Inactivity and Social Inclusion', *Working Brief*, Issue 132, Centre for Economic and Social Inclusion, March 2002
11 See note 8
12 R Exell, 'Employment and Poverty', in G Fimister (ed), *An End in Sight? Tackling child poverty in the UK*, Child Poverty Action Group, 2001
13 M Simic and S Sachin, 'People with Second Jobs', *Labour Market Trends*, Office for National Statistics, May 2002
14 P Kenway and G Palmer, *What do the Poverty Numbers Really Show?* Policy Analysis 3, New Policy Institute, 2002
15 *Facts about Low Pay, Rising Inequality: the great pay divide*, Low Pay Unit, 2001
16 See note 15
17 Minimum Wage Fact Sheet, Low Pay Unit, November 2001
18 See note 17
19 *Low Pay Estimates, Spring 2001*, Office for National Statistics, 24 January 2002
20 *Minimum Wage Enforcement*, Low Pay Unit, 2001
21 *The Changing Welfare State*, Social Security Spending, Department of Social Security, 2000
22 M Rahman, G Palmer and P Kenway, *Monitoring Poverty and Social Exclusion 2001*, New Policy Institute, Joseph Rowntree Foundation, 2001
23 M Brewer, T Clark and A Goodman, *The Government's Poverty Target: how much progress had been made?* Commentary 87, Institute for Fiscal Studies, 2002

24 *The Guardian, 8* April 2002

25 A Sinfield, 'The Problem of Riches', *Scottish Left Review*, Issue 6, September/October 2001

26 "Fat Cat' Pay Gap Continues to Rise – TUC Calls for Disclosure and Restraint', Press Release, TUC, 27 March 2002

27 See note 4

28 F Drever, K Fisher, J Brown and J Clark, *Social Inequalities 2000*, Office for National Statistics, 2000

29 See note 4

30 Rich List 2002, *Sunday Times*, 7 April 2002

31 A Harvey, 'Mind the Gap: widening inequalities and anti-poverty strategies', *Poverty*, 110, Autumn 2001, Child Poverty Action Group, 2001

# Four

# Groups vulnerable to poverty

The risks of poverty are not spread evenly, and they are dependent on a range of factors. These include: discrimination; the ability to meet the extra costs of a child, or those imposed by disability; unequal access to the labour market; geographical location; age; and gender. Also, the likelihood of experiencing poverty varies across the life cycle and over time. This section looks at some of the groups who are at risk of poverty. No group is homogenous; factors such as gender, disability, ethnicity and class need to be taken into account. Differences in income and education also exist both within and between groups. It should be noted that belonging to one of the groups mentioned below does not in itself cause poverty. Poverty is caused by the interaction of political, social, economic and personal factors.

## Women

Women are more likely to be poor than men and to remain in poverty for longer periods of time. They are vulnerable to poverty due to a combination of economic and social factors; a crucial one is their continuing role as primary carers for family. Many women have interrupted work histories and have to work in lower paid jobs to accommodate their family commitments, which can lead to poverty in later life. The two groups most at risk of poverty, lone parents and single pensioners, are predominately women.

There is a growing polarisation in women's experience. Those who have benefited from the expansion of education are most likely to see the greatest changes in their economic independence. Older women and those with few qualifications are more likely to be working than in the past but the potential for their economic independence is not nearly as great as that of their educated sisters.

## Employment and pay

The increasing number of women in the workforce, together with the growth of part-time employment, has had implications both for inequality and for poverty. It is no longer possible for families to rely on the 'male breadwinner' and the 'family wage'. *Households Below Average Income* (HBAI) data shows that 'two-earner' families have a much lower risk of poverty than households with only one earner.

The employment status of women in Scotland is similar to that which applies in the rest of the country; many more women are working full time, but the vast majority of part-time workers are still women (81.2 per cent). Women, especially between the ages of 25 and 54, are more likely than men to work part time. In 2000 in Scotland, 55.5 per cent of women worked full time and 44.5 per cent worked part time.

Women's jobs tend to be concentrated in certain occupations. In the UK 60 per cent of women work in just ten occupations.[1] There is some evidence that a high concentration of female employees is associated with

Table 4.1

**Percentage increases in weekly pay dispersions, 1997 and 2000, Scotland**

|  |  |  | 1997 | 2000 | % change |
|---|---|---|---|---|---|
| **Manual** | Male | bottom 10% | 180.00 | 198.80 | 10.4 |
|  |  | top 10% | 457.40 | 499.10 | 9.1 |
|  | Female | bottom 10% | 119.90 | 142.00 | 18.4 |
|  |  | top 10% | 284.50 | 308.10 | 8.2 |
| **Non-manual** | Male | bottom 10% | 211.20 | 230.60 | 9.2 |
|  |  | top 10% | 710.20 | 808.50 | 13.8 |
|  | Female | bottom 10% | 161.60 | 189.20 | 17.1 |
|  |  | top 10% | 445.20 | 508.80 | 14.3 |
| **All workers** | Male | bottom 10% | 192.30 | 213.00 | 10.8 |
|  |  | top 10% | 608.20 | 682.30 | 12.2 |
|  | Female | bottom 10% | 146.70 | 172.70 | 17.7 |
|  |  | top 10% | 435.10 | 485.90 | 11.7 |

Source: *Scottish Economic Statistics 2001* and *Poverty in Scotland 1999*

relatively low rates of pay. Women are still under-represented in higher paid jobs, and are also less likely to be self-employed.[2]

The pay gap between men's and women's wages has narrowed, but women's pay on average remains lower than men's. There is no single cause for the pay gap, but there is evidence that gender segregation in employment has a direct influence.[3] Between 1991 and 2001 the pay gap narrowed, but it is narrower at the lower end of the pay distribution than at the top end. The largest pay gap among major occupation groups in 2001 was for managers and administrators.[4]

Table 4.1 shows the increase in pay between 1997 and 2000 for the top and bottom deciles, for men and women in Scotland.

All workers have seen increases in pay, which have been greatest for the bottom 10 per cent of workers, particularly female workers, showing the positive effects of the national minimum wage. However, big differences in pay remain, as does the gender gap.

The top 10 per cent of female and male manual workers and the bottom 10 per cent of male manual workers had the lowest rises; this may reflect the fact that their wages were closest to the required legal levels.

In 2001 women's pay as a percentage of men's was 76.2 per cent, up by 1.5 per cent from the previous year.[5]

## Income

Men's individual income is generally higher than women's. A government study of individual income between 1996/97 and 1999/2000 found that the weekly median gross income for all men was more than twice that for all women. Over 40 per cent of all women had gross individual incomes of less than £100 per week, compared with less than 20 per cent of men.[6]

## Intra-household income

In many cases women benefit through shared household income. However, they are also more vulnerable to poverty within a household where there may not be an equitable distribution of resources or income. Moreover, women are also more likely to spend the income they receive directly on the family as, in most households, the responsibility for meeting children's needs is still seen as within the woman's domain.

Among the majority of couples, around 70 per cent of the gross family income comes from the man's individual income and 30 per cent from the woman's. The 70:30 ratio appears to be similar across all income bands. Only among 5 per cent of couples did the woman have a gross individual income of £200 per week or more and the man under £200. Differences in the level of income between men and women were smaller for single people.[7]

## Benefits

Women receive slightly higher benefit income than men. Benefit income accounts for 21 per cent of all women's weekly mean income, compared with 8 per cent for all men.[8] This is because women receive more dependants' benefits such as child benefit and working families' tax credit. Hence, benefit sanctions are likely to weigh much more heavily on women. For example, child benefit is paid to the main carer, usually the mother. For many women child benefit remains a significant part of their income. Proposals to cut the child benefit of parents of truants could impact disproportionately on some of the poorest women and children.

Table 4.2 shows a breakdown of key benefits by age group and gender in Scotland from 1995 to 2001.

Since 1995, key benefit take-up has fallen for both men and women, but male take-up fell more sharply. In 1995, 23 per cent of working-age men claimed key benefits, falling to 18 per cent in 2001. In comparison, in 1995, 18.4 per cent of women claimed key benefits, falling to 16.6 per cent in 2001.

In 2001, 13.1 per cent of 16–24-year-old women and 11.8 per cent of men claimed key benefits. Since 1998 there have been more women in this age group claiming key benefits.

There has been a steady decline in 25–64-year-old male key benefits claimants, from 24.3 per cent in 1995 to 19.3 per cent in 2001. The fall has been much smaller for female claimants, from 18.9 per cent in 1995 to 17.4 per cent in 2001.

Table 4.2

## Claimants of key benefits, by age group and gender, November 1995 to November 2001, Scotland

| | All | | Males | | Females | |
|---|---|---|---|---|---|---|
| | **000s** | **%** | **000s** | **%** | **000s** | **%** |
| **All ages** | | | | | | |
| 1995 | 662 | 20.8 | 380 | 23.0 | 282 | 18.4 |
| 1996 | 637 | 20.0 | 360 | 21.8 | 277 | 18.1 |
| 1997 | 600 | 18.9 | 331 | 20.1 | 269 | 17.6 |
| 1998 | 586 | 18.4 | 321 | 19.4 | 265 | 17.3 |
| 1999 | 575 | 18.0 | 312 | 18.8 | 263 | 17.2 |
| 2000 | 561 | 17.6 | 303 | 18.3 | 257 | 16.7 |
| 2001 | 553 | 17.3 | 298 | 18.0 | 255 | 16.6 |
| **Ages 16 to 24** | | | | | | |
| 1995 | 103 | 16.8 | 54 | 17.2 | 49 | 16.5 |
| 1996 | 92 | 15.5 | 48 | 15.6 | 45 | 15.3 |
| 1997 | 81 | 13.8 | 40 | 13.3 | 41 | 14.3 |
| 1998 | 77 | 13.3 | 38 | 12.9 | 39 | 13.9 |
| 1999 | 75 | 12.9 | 35 | 11.9 | 40 | 14.0 |
| 2000 | 71 | 12.3 | 33 | 11.2 | 38 | 13.4 |
| 2001 | 72 | 12.4 | 35 | 11.8 | 37 | 13.1 |
| **Ages 25 to 59/64** | | | | | | |
| 1995 | 559 | 21.7 | 326 | 24.3 | 233 | 18.9 |
| 1996 | 545 | 21.1 | 313 | 23.2 | 233 | 18.7 |
| 1997 | 519 | 20.0 | 291 | 21.6 | 228 | 18.3 |
| 1998 | 508 | 19.5 | 283 | 20.8 | 226 | 18.0 |
| 1999 | 500 | 19.2 | 277 | 20.4 | 224 | 7.9 |
| 2000 | 490 | 18.7 | 271 | 19.9 | 219 | 17.5 |
| 2001 | 481 | 18.4 | 263 | 19.3 | 218 | 17.4 |

Source: Client group analysis of IC (ASD)

Note: 'Key benefits' are jobseekers's allowance, incapacity benefit, severe disability allowance, disability living allowance and income support.

Table 4.3
## Pension provision by gender and age, 1999-2000, GB

|  | All aged 16 and over | 55-59 | 60-64 | 65 & over |
|---|---|---|---|---|
| **Males** |  |  |  |  |
| Occupational and/or personal pension | 61 | 70 | 51 | 4 |
| No pension scheme | 39 | 30 | 49 | 96 |
| **Females** |  |  |  |  |
| Occupational and/or personal pension | 52 | 55 | 37 | 2 |
| No pension scheme | 48 | 45 | 63 | 98 |

Source: Department of Social Security, *Family Resources Survey Great Britain 1999-2000*, 2001

## Pensions

Table 4.3 shows pension provision made by men and women in Great Britain.

Just under two-thirds of men contributed to occupational or personal pension schemes. Over a third did not have any pension provision.

Women's pension provision was more evenly split. Just over half had some form of pension provision and almost half had none. Only a third of women aged 60-64 had pension provision; 63 per cent of women in this age group had none compared with 49 per cent of men.

## Lone parents

The routes into lone parenthood are many and the characteristics of lone parent families are varied. The majority of lone-parent families result from divorce or separation.[9] Less than 3 per cent of all lone parents are under 20 years old; the average age of lone parents is 36 years.[10] Around a quarter of all families with dependent children are lone parents. There are over 162,000 lone parents in Scotland; the majority (93 per cent) are women.[11]

## Lone parents and poverty

Lone parents are disproportionately represented among those who face poverty. They are twice as likely to be poor as compared with couples with children. Over half (54 per cent) of lone-parent households are poor; around three-quarters are in the bottom two quintiles. Lone-parent families are also more likely to experience persistent low income.[12] Lone-parent poverty results mainly because they tend to be solely responsible for both the financial and practical commitments of their family.

## Employment

In the UK there has been an increase in the number of lone parents in work, from 44 per cent in 1997 to 51 per cent in 2001.[13] In 2001 (Autumn) in the UK, around 45 per cent of lone parents were unemployed.[14] Lone mothers with children under five are less likely to work than mothers in couples; 32 per cent compared with 60 per cent.[15] Lack of qualifications remains a barrier for many lone parents. Over a third of them and nearly half of those not in work (44 per cent) have no academic qualifications.[16] The main barriers to work for lone parents are the cost and availability of childcare, illness or disability of a child, lack of opportunities for work and low levels of skill and confidence.[17]

The New Deal for lone parents is designed to increase the proportion of lone parents in work to 70 per cent over ten years. It is now compulsory for all lone parents on income support to attend regular work-based interviews. Paid work can of course improve the financial circumstances of lone parents, but employment often creates additional expenses such as the costs of childcare, transport and work clothes, with the result that some lone parents may not be better off in work.[18]

Research for the Department for Work and Pensions found that one in five non-working lone parents had a health problem and one in ten had a child with health problems that restricted their opportunities to work.[19] Moreover, while many of the Government's initiatives are intended to give groups such as lone parents greater financial security, the emphasis is on paid work, and that only deals with part of the picture. Many lone parents have sole responsibility for their children and may have other family commitments. This 'unpaid work' is not recognised in current government policy. But the unpaid work of caring is one of the major causes of women's poverty. In effect, ignoring unpaid work can result in indirect discrimination.

## Benefits

In August 2001 in Scotland, 79,000 lone parents claimed key benefits: 18.8 per cent of income support claimants were lone parents. Around 47 per cent of those who claimed had a child less than five years old.[20] Benefit income accounted for just under half of the gross individual income for single women with children; 43 per cent of mean benefit income was derived from dependant benefits.[21]

## Childcare

There is evidence that affordable childcare is a major factor in poverty reduction for families. It increases access to the labour force and waged income for parents, especially lone mothers. The education, health and welfare of children, particularly young children, can also benefit from good quality childcare. Government recognition of these facts, and its commitment to work-based solutions to family poverty have led to a variety of policies and programmes to boost childcare as part of an anti-poverty strategy in Scotland.

Childcare places have increased. All three-year-olds are now entitled to two and a half hours of pre-school education. Private and voluntary sector daycare has multiplied, and out-of-school care has mushroomed. The rate of increase (excluding childminders) varies for different ages. Between 1997 and 2001 in Scotland there appears to have been an increase of just

Table 4.4

**Help towards childcare costs under family credit (FC, August 1999) and working families' tax credit (WFTC, November 2001)**

|  | Aug 1999 | Nov 2001 |
|---|---|---|
|  | FC | WFTC |
| Number awards including help with childcare | 45,400 | 159,415 |
| Percentage awards that included help with childcare | 6% | 12% |
| Average FC childcare disregard | £22.08 | £39 (GB) |
| Average WFTC childcare allowance award |  | £36 (UK) |

Source: Inland Revenue Analysis and Research, *Working Families' and Disabled Person's Tax Credit Statistics: geographical analysis*, Office for National Statistics, 2001

less than 10 per cent for under eight-year-olds, compared with an increase of 30 per cent of places for over eight-year-olds.

One of the major means of re-directing funds to childcare has been the working families' tax credit childcare allowance. Working families' tax credit (WFTC) is more generous than family credit, which it replaced. It pays 70 per cent of the actual costs of childcare incurred by working parents. As can be seen from Table 4.4, proportionately and numerically, many more working parents are benefiting from the help towards childcare costs offered by WFTC.

Of those benefiting from the childcare element of WFTC, 90 per cent are lone parents, suggesting it has brought real help to those who cannot look to another partner to undertake childcare if they find work. Even though 11 per cent of WFTC claimants are receiving help with childcare costs, this is only a quarter of those thought to be entitled to such help.

The primary reason for the low take-up is still the lack of good quality, affordable childcare, especially in deprived areas. A number of strategies are being developed to address the problem. They include funding by a variety of agencies such as New Opportunities Fund, local enterprise companies, employment programmes and the Childcare Strategy to support new childcare services. But perversely, because these services are required to become economically self-sufficient, their fees may become too expensive for the low-income families they have been created to assist, even with the help of WFTC.

There is growing concern that the expansion of childcare, being largely market and area-based, is inappropriate as a model for integrating childcare and anti-poverty strategies. Critics call attention to the plethora of funders and programmes of childcare development, competition between different providers, prioritising the needs of the economy over the needs of children, and the lack of strategic development in the country. In many ways it might be easier to follow a more generous and publicly-funded route to increasing childcare for low-income households.

## Disability

As a group, people with disabilities are at greater risk of poverty than non-disabled people. Around a fifth of the adult population in Scotland (800,000) are disabled; two-thirds of them are over 60. Over half (59 per cent) of all disabled people are women.[22]

Discrimination, both personal and institutional, can limit job opportunities for disabled people. For example, employers may believe that they are not capable of doing particular jobs, or be unwilling to make necessary adaptations to the workplace or to working practices. Similarly, lack of access to public buildings and transport – for example 35 per cent of railway stations in Scotland have inaccessible platforms[23] – may limit a person's ability to engage in employment and many other everyday pursuits. Low incomes combined with unequal access to education, transport, leisure and other services mean that disabled people are often unable to participate fully in society. Such exclusion may extend to other family members, particularly those with the main responsibility for caring.

In April 2000, the Disability Rights Commission was established. It is an independent body whose aim is to eliminate discrimination against the disabled and promote equality of opportunity. It monitors the implementation of the Disability Discrimination Act.

## Incidence of poverty

People with disabilities are over-represented in low-income groups. Families with one or more disabled persons are more likely to be living in poverty. Working-age adults who are disabled or have a disabled partner make up around one-third of households below the poverty thresholds.[24] Table 4.5 shows the proportion of households in Scotland with and without a disabled person, within various income bands in 1999.

In 1999 there was a greater percentage of households with disabled people in the lower income bands. Over two-thirds of such households had incomes of £10,000 or less.

Nineteen per cent of households with no disabled person had incomes of £20,000 or more, compared with only 6 per cent of households with a disabled person.

## Benefits

There are over 2.6 million disabled people out of work and on benefits in Great Britain; disabled people are almost eight times as likely as non-disabled people to be in this position. They are also more likely to be receiving in-work benefits.[25] In November 2001 in Scotland, 30 per cent of income support claimants were disabled; Scotland has a higher percent-

Table 4.5

**Percentage of households (column percentages) with/without a disabled person living in them, by income group, 1999, Scotland**

|  | % households with a disabled person | % households with no disabled person |
|---|---|---|
| £6,000 or under | 32 | 26 |
| £6,001 – £10,000 | 35 | 24 |
| £10,001 – £15,000 | 20 | 19 |
| £15,001 – £20,000 | 7 | 12 |
| Over £20,000 | 6 | 19 |
| All | 100 | 100 |

Source: *Scottish Household Survey*, Bulletin 2, Scottish Executive, 1999

age of disabled claimants of key benefits than the Great Britain average.[26]

Severe disablement allowance was a non-contributory benefit aimed at people who had never worked or not been able to pay sufficient national insurance contributions to receive incapacity benefit. People over 20 years of age could only get severe disablement allowance if they were judged as 80 per cent or more disabled. In April 2001, this benefit was abolished for new claimants. However, some people who were already claiming the benefit will continue to receive it. In May 2001, there were over 42,000 claimants of severe disablement allowance in Scotland.[27]

The majority of benefits designed specifically for disabled people are not means-tested, and in some cases may be paid to someone in work. The various benefits are overlapping and inconsistent, and often result in inadequate provision. The Government is now taking an 'active approach' to the management of disability benefits.[28] There is particular concern to move claimants of incapacity benefit into work and further limits have been set to the eligibility criteria for incapacity benefits.

## Employment

Disabled people are only half as likely as non-disabled people to be in employment. In Scotland in 2001, there were 254,000 disabled people in employment; this is 40 per cent of all working-age long-term disabled people. There is evidence that on average, disabled people in work are more likely to stay in the same job than non-disabled people.[29] International Labour Organisation (ILO) unemployment rates for long-term disabled people are nearly twice as high as for non-disabled people.[30]

The New Deal for disabled people is primarily focused on people in receipt of incapacity benefits; currently it has no compulsory elements. In Scotland at the end January 2002, there were 1,194 disabled people participating in the 18–24-year-old New Deal, and 1,690 in the 25+ New Deal.[31]

Disabled people are twice as likely as non-disabled people to have no qualifications. The difference is consistent across all age groups: Table 4.6 shows the numbers and percentage of long-term disabled people of working age who have no qualifications in Great Britain.

Table 4.6

**Long-term disabled adults of working age with no qualifications (row percentages), 1999/2000, thousands and percentages, GB**

|  | Long-term disabled | | All of working age | |
| --- | --- | --- | --- | --- |
|  | 000s | % | 000s | % |
| 16-24 years | 142 | 23 | 937 | 15 |
| 25-34 years | 199 | 19 | 768 | 9 |
| 35-49 years | 598 | 26 | 1855 | 15 |
| 50-59/64 years | 1022 | 37 | 2198 | 26 |
| All aged 16-59/64 | 1962 | 29 | 5759 | 16 |

Source: Disability Rights Commission, *Disability Briefing*, 2001. Original data source: Labour Force Survey, Winter 1999/00

In 1999/00 in Great Britain, over a quarter (29 per cent) of working-age long-term disabled adults had no qualifications, compared with 16 per cent of all working-age adults.

## Extra costs

Disabled people face a number of extra costs. Disability covers a wide range of circumstances, so any assessment of extra costs should address individual needs. The extra costs which a disabled person might incur include: needs specific to the disability, for example, transport, medicines or food; one-off costs such as housing-related items or adaptations; and enhanced costs for common needs which are higher for a disabled person. There may also be extra costs for basic items, for example, when it is necessary to shop locally because transport problems prevent people from getting to distant but cheaper supermarkets. Costs associated with working may significantly decrease the financial benefits of employment.

The majority of disabled people do not receive any extra-costs benefits. For those who cannot meet such costs from earnings or additional sources of income or who rely on benefits, the absence of help with extra costs is likely to push them into poverty.

## Ethnic minorities

While the causes of poverty within minority ethnic communities are similar to those affecting the white population, the additional dimension of racial discrimination is likely to exacerbate the overall experience of poverty. Information about ethnic minorities in Scotland is still scarce, and the Scottish Executive and the UK government are taking steps to improve this situation. Available data is of variable quality and inconsistent in its coverage of different minority ethnic communities.

## Income

Overall rates of poverty are higher for all minority ethnic households in comparison to white households:

> 'Individuals in households headed by a member of an ethnic minority community were skewed towards the bottom of the income distribution.'[32]

Poverty rates vary between different ethnic groups. Table 4.7 shows the proportion of households by ethnic group below the 50 per cent mean and 60 per cent median thresholds.

Over two-thirds of Pakistani/Bangladeshi households and around half of Black non-Caribbean households are poor. Over three out of five individuals in Pakistani and Bangladeshi groups have incomes in the bottom quintile of the income distribution.[33]

Table 4.7

**Percentage of individuals in low-income households (row percentages), by ethnic group of head of household (after housing costs and including self-employed), 2000/01, UK**

|  | Below 50% mean | Below 60% median | All individuals (millions) |
|---|---|---|---|
| White | 22 | 21 | 52.7 |
| Black Caribbean | 34 | 31 | 0.7 |
| Black non-Caribbean | 51 | 49 | 0.5 |
| Indian | 32 | 30 | 1.0 |
| Pakistani/Bangladeshi | 69 | 68 | 1.0 |
| Other | 37 | 36 | 1.0 |

Source: Department for Work and Pensions, *Households Below Average Income 2000/01*, 2002, Table 3.5

## Employment and low pay

Minority ethnic communities are, in general, concentrated in areas where employment opportunities are now low or are working in the 'types of jobs that are declining in number and relative income'.[34] In Scotland the majority of ethnic minority workers originally worked either in the public sector or in catering and retailing. With privatisation, cuts in public services and changes in retailing, many of the traditional routes into work are being closed. Self-employment is more common in Scotland amongst ethnic minorities than in the white community.

Many people from minority ethnic communities work in sectors where low wages are common. The Low Pay Commission has noted that ethnic minority employees are over-represented in low-paid jobs.[35] This is particularly true for Pakistani and Bangladeshi workers.

There are differences both between and within different minority ethnic communities. There is evidence that within some minority ethnic groups a significant proportion goes on to higher paid, higher status jobs. For example, 5 per cent of Indian men are doctors, a rate ten times higher than for white men. However, this movement often masks the 'lack of progress of others within that group'.[36] This polarisation is described as 'forking', and has been found to exist within both the Indian and Black African communities.[37]

# Unemployment

In spite of improvements in the employment situation, unemployment remains high for all minority ethnic groups. One of the Scottish Executive's targets is to increase the employment rates for ethnic minorities.[38] At the end of January 2002 in Scotland, there were 180 people from minority ethnic communities participating in the 18–24 New Deal and 83 in the 25+ New Deal.[39] The number of people from minority ethnic communities taking part in the Labour Force Survey in Scotland is too small to produce a reliable picture, so we use UK figures.

Table 4.8

**Economic activity by ethnic group, 2002, UK**

|  | Economic activity rate | Employment rate | ILO unemployment rate |
|---|---|---|---|
|  | (ages 16-59/64) | | all ages 16+ |
| White | 79.4 | 75.9 | 4.4 |
| All minority ethnic groups | 64.7 | 57.4 | 11.1 |
| Mixed | 70.0 | 62.2 | 11.1 |
| Asian | 61.9 | 55.4 | 10.6 |
| Black | 71.1 | 61.8 | 12.9 |
| Chinese | 58.3 | 54.1 | * |
| Other ethnic groups | 58.3 | 52.8 | 9.2 |

Source: National Statistics, *Labour Force Survey, Quarterly Supplement*, February 2002, Table 10
Sample size too small for reliable estimate.*

The unemployment rate for all minority ethnic groups is more than double the rate of that of white individuals. Pakistani and Bangladeshi groups have the highest rates of unemployment.

# Discrimination

Discrimination on the grounds of race is illegal in the UK, but it still occurs. Many institutions in our society also operate in ways that effectively discriminate against ethnic minorities. Racism is a consistent factor in the lives of people from minority ethnic communities. Racist incidents range

from name-calling, graffiti, spitting and stoning, through to physical violence and murder. In 1999/2000 Scottish police recorded 2,200 racist
incidents.[40] But this is likely to be a gross underestimation: the Commission for Racial Equality estimates that only 5 per cent of incidents are
reported to the police.[41] The consequences of racial harassment are
severe; it impacts on family relations, interactions with the wider community and health. A study on racist victimisation noted:

> 'the impact on health and wellbeing was quite profound. The majority of
> people were not physically attacked but the consequences of racist victimi-
> sation had changed their lives.'[42]

## Benefits

Access to benefits is not an easy option for people from minority ethnic
communities. A number of factors such as immigration laws, language
problems and racism contribute to creating discrimination within the social
security system. Information on benefit take-up by ethnicity is not generally available for Scotland. Figure 4.9 below shows benefit take-up, by
ethnic group in Great Britain.

Fewer older people from minority ethnic communities receive pensions, as many began work in this country in the middle of their working
lives; moreover they often worked in low-paid jobs and could not build up
the necessary entitlement.

The higher uptake of benefits, such as income support, by
Pakistani, Bangladeshi and Black households reflects the high unemployment and poverty within these groups.

Child benefit is higher for all ethnic minorities, reflecting the younger
profile of these households.

## Older people

In 2000 there were 924,000 older people in Scotland. The older population is estimated to increase from 17.9 per cent in 1998 to 24 per cent of
the total population in 2036.[43]

Poverty for older people reflects the circumstances of their working
lives. If they were unemployed for long periods, worked in low-paid jobs,

Table 4.9

## Percentage of benefit units for a selection of benefits, by ethnic group of head of household, 1999/2000, GB

|  | White | Black | Indian | Pakistani | Bangladeshi |
|---|---|---|---|---|---|
| Family credit/working families' tax credit | 2 | 4 | 4 | 8 | 3 |
| Income support | 10 | 19 | 14 | 22 | 16 |
| Housing benefit | 14 | 28 | 9 | 19 | 19 |
| Council tax benefit | 18 | 29 | 15 | 29 | 20 |
| Retirement pension | 25 | 13 | 8 | 6 | 6 |
| Jobseeker's allowance | 3 | 8 | 4 | 9 | 4 |
| Incapacity benefit | 5 | 2 | 4 | 3 | 2 |
| Disability living allowance (care) | 4 | 3 | 3 | 6 | 2 |
| Disability living allowance (mobility) | 5 | 4 | 3 | 5 | 3 |
| Child benefit | 22 | 30 | 34 | 42 | 27 |
| On any benefit | 59 | 60 | 55 | 62 | 49 |
| No benefits | 41 | 40 | 45 | 38 | 51 |

Source: Department of Social Security, *Family Resources Survey Great Britain 1999-2000*, 2001, Table 3.17.

Note: Benefit units refer to a single adult or couple living as married and any dependent children.

Table 4.10

## Numbers and percentages of pensioners in low-income households (after housing costs), 1994/95-2000/01, UK

|  | All pensioners (millions) | Below 50% mean | | Below 60% median | |
|---|---|---|---|---|---|
|  |  | (millions) | (% of all pensioners) | (millions) | (% of all pensioners) |
| 1994/95 | 9.6 | 2.6 | 27 | 2.5 | 26 |
| 1995/96 | 9.5 | 2.6 | 27 | 2.4 | 25 |
| 1996/97 | 9.4 | 2.6 | 28 | 2.5 | 27 |
| 1997/98 | 9.5 | 2.7 | 29 | 2.6 | 27 |
| 1998/99 | 9.5 | 2.9 | 30 | 2.6 | 27 |
| 1999/00 | 9.5 | 2.6 | 28 | 2.4 | 26 |
| 2000/01 | 9.5 | 2.6 | 27 | 2.3 | 25 |

Source: Department for Work and Pensions, *Households Below Average Income 2000/01*, 2002

had insecure or interrupted work histories, were ill for long periods, or involved in unpaid work, they are more likely to be poor. This is because they are unlikely to have occupational pensions or savings, and they are dependent on state benefits. Many may also have reduced benefit entitlement. Table 4.10 shows the numbers of pensioners below the 50 per cent mean and the 60 per cent median thresholds.

In 2000/01 in the UK, 27 per cent of all pensioners (2.6 million) lived in households with incomes below 50 per cent of the average income threshold. Between 1997 and 1999 there was a rise in pensioner poverty; this appears to have stopped. The current position is the same as it was in 1994/95.

There has been a decrease in the number of pensioners with incomes below the 60 per cent median threshold. In 2000/01, a quarter of pensioners in the UK (2.3 million) lived on incomes below this threshold. Pensioners are also more likely to be persistently poor.

## Benefits

In 1999/2000 in the UK, 70 per cent of pensioners depended on a state pension for at least half their income.[44] The Government is to introduce a 'pension credit' in 2003 to ensure that people's income does not fall below a specified income level. Rules of entitlement will be more generous. There is also an element to reward those who have savings or occupational pensions. This 'top up' component will be index-linked to earnings. It will replace the minimum income guarantee and be administered by the Department for Work and Pensions.

There are concerns that the more generous provision is tied to an increase in means-testing. Many older people do not claim means-tested benefits even when they are entitled to them. The Government's own figures show that in 1999/2000, between 22 and 36 per cent of pensioners entitled to income support did not claim it.[45]

Table 4.11 shows the numbers and percentage of people in Scotland on retirement pension and other key benefits.

Table 4.11

## Claimants of retirement pensions and other key benefits, May 2001, Scotland

| | All | | Males | | Females | |
|---|---|---|---|---|---|---|
| | **000s** | **%** | **000s** | **%** | **000s** | **%** |
| Retirement pension only | 622.2 | 67.4 | 234.0 | 73.5 | 388.2 | 64.1 |
| Retirement pension, disability living allowance | 49.1 | 5.3 | 19.7 | 6.2 | 29.4 | 4.9 |
| Retirement pension, attendance allowance | 76.1 | 8.2 | 26.6 | 8.4 | 49.4 | 8.2 |
| Retirement pension, disability allowance, attendance allowance | 1.4 | 0.1 | 0.6 | 0.2 | 0.8 | 0.1 |
| Retirement pension, income support | 70.3 | 7.6 | 15.7 | 4.9 | 54.5 | 9.0 |
| Retirement pension, income support, disability living allowance | 20.9 | 2.3 | 7.0 | 2.2 | 14.0 | 2.3 |
| Retirement pension, income support, attendance allowance | 56.2 | 6.1 | 10.8 | 3.4 | 45.4 | 7.5 |
| Retirement pension, income support, disability living allowance, attendance allowance | 0.7 | 0.1 | 0.2 | 0.1 | 0.5 | 0.1 |
| All | 912.8 | 98.8 | 318.0 | 99.9 | 594.8 | 98.2 |

Source: Client Group Analysis Over State Pension Age, 31 May 2001, and Population Estimates Unit, Office for National Statistics and Scottish Registrar.

In May 2001 in Scotland, over two-thirds of all pensioners claimed retirement pension. There were more male claimants (73.5 per cent) than female (64.1 per cent).

Almost twice as many women (9.0 per cent) as men (4.9 per cent) claimed retirement pension and income support.

Around 8 per cent of all pensioners claimed retirement pension and attendance allowance. However, more women claimed these benefits in conjunction with income support.

## Income and spending

Average net income after housing costs for pensioners in 1999/2000 was £180 per week. Single pensioners had lower incomes (£126 per week) than pensioner couples (£263 per week). Single female pensioners had average net incomes of £119 per week compared with £149 per week for male pensioners. Those over 75 years receive less than those under 75.[46] Analysis of individual income by the Cabinet shows that between 1996/67 and 1999/2000, married women pensioners had the lowest median individual income.[47] Average income for the top fifth of pensioners was more than three times that of the bottom fifth in 1999/2000. The median net income (after housing costs) for pensioner couples in the bottom fifth was £114, compared with £449 for the top fifth.[48]

Pensioner households tend to spend a higher proportion of money on housing, fuel and food. In 1999/2000, households in which the head was aged 65 or over spent around 40 per cent of income on these items compared with 36 per cent in other households. In households where pensioners were mainly dependent on state pensions nearly 48 per cent was spent on these essentials.[49] It is a matter of concern that pensioners have less money to meet their social and psychological needs; to the detriment of their well-being.

## Pension provision

In order to reduce poverty in later life, the Government is keen to increase the numbers of people who contribute to a non-state pension. But a survey by MORI found that more than a quarter of people in Great Britain aged 16 to 64 say they have not really thought about saving for retirement or paying into a pension. Only one in five is confident that they will have sufficient income in retirement and only half are making provision. The report notes 'there is much confusion about what sort of provision people should be making for their retirement and how much they should be setting aside.'[50]

Among those who *are* saving for retirement, confidence in private insurance has been shaken by recent mismanagement in the pension industry. Figure 4.1 shows the proportion of working-age people in Scotland who contributed to non-state pensions, from 1994/95 to 1998/99.

Figure 4.1

**Proportion of working-age people contributing to a non-state pension, 1994/95-1998/99, Scotland**

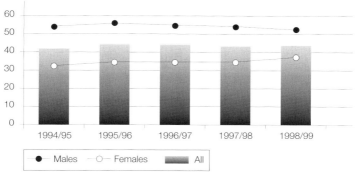

Source: Scottish Executive, *Social Justice: Annual Report 2001*, Table 20b. Original source: Department for Work and Pensions, *Family Resources Survey*.

Overall, less than half of working-age people contributed to non-state pensions in Scotland in this period, during which time there was a slight increase in women's contributions and a small decrease in men's contributions.

# Young people

Young people's poverty is often concealed by household circumstances, particularly when they must remain in the parental home because they cannot afford to move, or when their personal income may be adequate, but the household in which they live, and to which they must contribute, is poor. Information on young people in Scotland remains patchy; there is more information on their criminal behaviour than on employment or low pay. We have used Scottish statistics where possible, otherwise UK statistics are quoted.

## Unemployment

Unemployment among young people (18 to 24 years old) has fallen, but it is twice as high as that of older workers.[51]

Table 4.12 shows the employment status of young people in Scotland in 2001.

Table 4.12

**Employment status of young people (16–24-year-olds), 2001, Scotland**

|                              | Males | Females | All  |
| ---------------------------- | ----- | ------- | ---- |
| In employment (000s)         | 179   | 170     | 349  |
| Employment rate              | 62%   | 61%     | 61%  |
| ILO unemployed (000s)        | 37    | 16      | 53   |
| Unemployment rate            | 17%   | 9%      | 13%  |
| Economically active (000s)   | 216   | 186     | 402  |
| Economic activity rate       | 75%   | 66%     | 71%  |
| Outside labour market        | 73    | 94      | 167  |

Source: Equal Opportunities Commission Scotland, *Facts about Women and Men in Scotland*, 2002

Note: Employment rate = in employment as percentage of economically active + outside labour market; unemployment rate = ILO unemployed as percentage of in employment; economic activity rate = economically active as percentage of economically active + outside labour market.

In 2001 in Scotland, 61 per cent of young people were in employment, while 13 per cent were ILO unemployed. There were more unemployed men (17 per cent) than women (9 per cent). Three quarters of young men and two-thirds of young women were economically active.

Those categorised as outside the labour market include young people who are still at school, or are in further or higher education, and those who are sick or disabled, or undertaking caring duties. There are more women than men in this group.

In Scotland between December 2001 and February 2002 there has been an increase in the employment rate for 16–17-year-olds. The increase was higher for young women.

The employment rate for 18–24-year-olds fell from 68.1 per cent in

November 2001 to 64.9 per cent in February 2002. The fall was higher for young men (–6.6) than for young women (–2.4).[52]

## Low pay

The introduction of the national minimum wage improved pay rates for younger people. However the New Policy Institute notes that the numbers of young people earning below half median earnings (the slightly more generous threshold) have not decreased to any great extent. In 2000, half a million young adults between 18 and 21 years earned less than £4 an hour (the half median threshold for that year). While the minimum wage has had an effect on the worst pay excesses, 'low pay remains a major problem among young adults which has not yet been fully resolved.'[53] The Low Pay Commission has consistently recommended that 21-year-olds should be entitled to the adult rate.[54]

## New Deal

The New Deal for young people was introduced in April 1998. It is compulsory for all 18–24-year-olds who have been unemployed for at least six months. It aims to help young unemployed people into jobs and increase their employability. Between January 1998 and January 2002 in Scotland, 85,520 young people entered the New Deal and 75,300 left the programme. Since the New Deal scheme began, in Scotland 40,700 young people on it have gone into jobs.[55]

A report by the National Audit Commission on the New Deal for young people found evidence of improvements in the long-term employability of participants, but noted:

> 'The Employment Service has not been able to monitor systematically the nature and quality of jobs achieved by New Deal for young people participants, their progress once made in employment or increase in their employability.'

The report recommended a greater focus on the needs of those with severe or multiple barriers to employment.[56]

There remain concerns about the use of benefit penalties in conjunction with New Deal programmes. In Britain (October-December 2001 quarter) 3,235 sanctions were imposed. Environmental schemes have the largest numbers of those sanctioned. In Scotland in this period around 31 per cent of those on such schemes faced sanctions.[57] Many of those sanctioned 'have a high prevalence of problems and multiple barriers to getting to work'.[58]

In 2001 in Britain, 160,000 of 16–18-year-olds were not employed or in education or training. This number has changed little since 1993.[59] In 2001 in Scotland, around 14 per cent of 16–19-year-olds were not in employment, training or education. The proportion of young people in this position has remained between 13 and 16 per cent since 1992.[60] Around a quarter (24.3 per cent) of those entering New Deal in Scotland had no qualifications. As the information was supplied by participants and over a third did not respond, this is likely to be an under-estimation of the number of young people with no qualifications.[61]

Table 4.13

**Percentage of 16–19-year-olds not in education, training or employment, 1992-2001, Scotland**

| 1992 | 14 |
|------|----|
| 1993 | 15 |
| 1994 | 16 |
| 1995 | 16 |
| 1996 | 14 |
| 1997 | 13 |
| 1998 | 14 |
| 1999 | 13 |
| 2000 | 14 |
| 2001 | 14 |

Source: Office for National Statistics, *Labour Force Survey*, 2001

## Benefits

Young people under 25 are not eligible for the same rates of benefit as people aged 25 or over. Those aged 18–24 may only claim reduced rates of income support, while young people aged 16–17 have no automatic entitlement to benefit, but can claim only in very restricted circumstances.

Figure 4.2
**Jobseeker's allowance recipients aged 16-17, November 1996 to November 2001, Scotland**

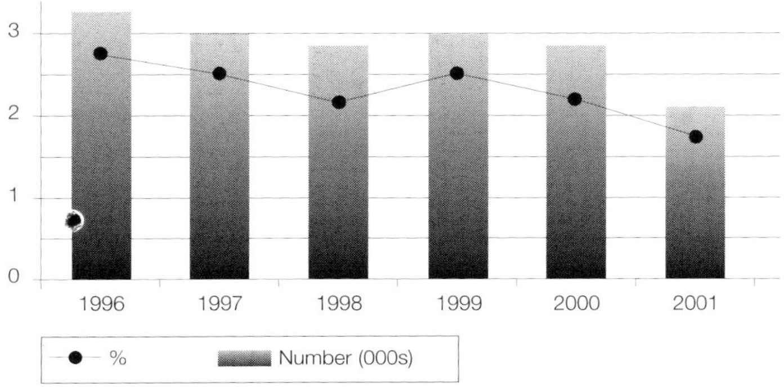

Source: Department of Work and Pensions, Analytical Services Directorate Information Centre, Newcastle upon Tyne, May 2002.

Figure 4.2 shows the number of 16–17-year-old jobseeker's allowance (JSA) claimants in Scotland between 1992 and 2001.

In Scotland, 3,400 16–17-year-olds claimed JSA in November 1996. This fell to 2,100 in November 2001.

Since 1999 there has been a slow drop in the numbers of 16/17-year-old JSA claimants.

In 2001 around 12.4 per cent of 16–24-year-olds claimed key benefits. There has been a steady decline in the numbers and percentage of claimants since 1995.

# Geographic areas

Whilst most of the data in this book relates to Scotland and the UK as a whole, there is a danger that information based on averages and overall totals will conceal the degrees of differences in wealth, poverty and deprivation. Moreover, even when data is more localised, differences can be obscured. For example, capital cities such as Edinburgh and London tend to perform well on indicators such as employment and income, but there are areas within them where indices show high unemployment and poverty. Spatial and social segregation often go together. These are often obscured in the overall totals.

It is not possible to provide here a complete picture of the geographic variations in disadvantage and deprivation in Scotland, but their existence should be taken into account when considering poverty. Brief notes are provided below, covering some issues and factors of relevance and a number of essays in Section 3 also make reference to these issues.

## Information

Initiatives such as the Scottish Neighbourhood Statistics project and the Scottish Household Survey mean that a great deal more information on Scotland will be available in the future, and there is already more than before devolution. The Scottish Neighbourhood Statistics project, for example, has a budget of £7 million over three years from 2001. The aim of the project is to make a major contribution to social justice and area regeneration programmes by collecting and making understandable information available on health, education, poverty, unemployment, housing, population, equalities and social/community issues, on a unit postcode basis whenever possible. (More information can be found on the website at www.scotland.gov.uk/stats/neighbours/ tables/neighbours.asp)

## Rural poverty

Poverty may be most frequently associated with urban settings, but this disguises the fact that it is also prevalent in many rural areas:

> 'Because the rural areas do not tend to have the same concentrations of people experiencing disadvantage that may be seen in large urban centres, the severity of rural problems may be overlooked.'[62]

Information on rural poverty is limited and often difficult to find: smaller populations, scattered communities and large geographical areas exacerbate the problems of data collection.

The population of rural Scotland is just under 1.5 million. It is estimated that there are around 26,000 multiply deprived households and 2,500 severely deprived households in rural Scotland.[63]

Differences exist both within and between rural areas in terms of the availability of and variability of employment. At present, rapid industrial change is a marked feature of both rural and urban contexts. However, for rural areas, the sudden closure of a large plant or changes in particular industries such as textiles or agriculture may have a widespread effect, which the local economy finds more difficult to absorb. Even so, unemployment tends to be lower in rural areas. The Scottish Household Survey Bulletin 6 found, for example, that adults in 'accessible small towns' and 'accessible rural' areas are most likely to be in some form of employment (56 per cent and 57 per cent respectively), with adults in 'the four cities' least likely (47 per cent). Glasgow has the lowest proportion of adults in employment (39 per cent) and the Lothians have the highest (56 per cent).[64] However, there is evidence that official statistics underestimate unemployment in rural areas. Low pay and limited employment opportunities remain issues of concern in particular, as the cost of living tends to be higher in rural areas.

Poor service provision and the increasing necessity to travel in order to get access to basic services may exacerbate poverty and social exclusion in rural areas. At the same time, the lack of public transport means that people are dependent on private car use, so for those people who have little or no access to private transport, the availability of basic public services and leisure facilities is limited.

## Area regeneration

There is a spatial concentration of poverty within particular localities in the UK, and anti-poverty strategies over the last decade have tended to be area-based. In comparison with the rest of the UK, Scotland is placed within the mid-range of a number of indices, but there are areas of Scotland, particularly within Glasgow, which are ranked amongst the poorest in the UK. According to the 1998 Scottish Deprivation Index, 22 out of the 25 most deprived postcode areas of Scotland are in Glasgow.[65] Households in Edinburgh are more likely than households in the other local authority groups to say they are 'managing very well' or 'managing quite well' financially (48 per cent), while households in Glasgow are least likely to say this (28 per cent). They also report that neighbourhood problems are seen as most common in 'the four cities', followed by 'other urban areas' and then 'small accessible towns'.[66]

Economic and social change and the direction of social policy have produced winners and losers. Urban policy has many critics, not least from within communities themselves as they struggle to make sense of top-down policies and vie for short term funding. But the 1990s saw a growing emphasis on partnerships between residents and professionals and policy integration through strategies such as the UK's *Bringing Britain Together: a New Deal for Communities* and Scotland's *Social Inclusion Strategy: Opening the Door to a Better Scotland* (1999). The Scottish social inclusion partnership areas are similar to the neighbourhood regeneration areas of England and Wales. In England and Wales government social inclusion work is co-ordinated through the Social Exclusion Unit, which is attached to the Cabinet Office. In Scotland, social inclusion policy is informed by the Scottish Social Inclusion Network. The Scottish Executive contributes funding for 36 area-based and 14 thematic social inclusion partnerships to 'tackle injustice and exclusion at local level, in urban and rural areas'. In 1999 the Scottish Executive selected the areas for additional funding according to criteria of social need and bid quality.

The need for strategies that take account of locality and grouping should not obscure the fact that there are a number of common factors that are relevant. Health and education services that are accessible and efficient, the availability of decent employment, affordable good quality childcare, leisure services and transport and an adequate income are all factors that have to be achieved in order to overcome poverty and deprivation, wherever the locality.

## Notes

1   *Understanding the Gender Pay Gap*, Women and Equality Unit, 2002
2   See note 1
3   'Women's Pay in Europe', *Labour Market Trends*, Office for National Statistics, May 2002
4   'Labour Market Spotlight', *Labour Market Trends*, Office for National Statistics, May 2002
5   'Equal Pay a Lifetime Away?' Press Release, Transport and General Workers Union, 8 March 2002
6   Cabinet Office, *Individuals' Income 1996/97–1999/2000*, Office for National Statistics, 2001
7   See note 6
8   See note 6
9   *Labour Force Survey*, Office for National Statistics, 2001
10  A Marsh, S McKay, A Smith and A Stephenson, *Low-income Families in Britain*,

Research Report No138, Department for Work and Pensions, 2001

11 *Social Trends 30*, Office for National Statistics, 2000

12 *Households Below Average Income 2000/01*, Department for Work and Pensions, 2002

13 *Lone Parents and Employment: the facts*, National Council for One Parent Families, 2001

14 *Work and Worklessness Among Households*, Autumn 2001, Office for National Statistics, January 2002

15 See note 13

16 See note 13

17 *One-parent Families Today*, National Council for One Parent Families, 2001

18 J Casebourne, 'A Better Deal for Lone Parents', *Working Brief*, Issue 131, Centre for Economic and Social Inclusion, 2002

19 A Marsh and K Rowlingson, *Low/Moderate-income Families in Britain: changes in 1999-2000*, Research Report No 165, Department for Work and Pensions, 2002

20 One Plus, *Annual Review*, 2001

21 See note 6

22 S Riddell and P Banks, *Disability in Scotland 2001: key facts and figures*, Disability Rights Commission, 2001

23 See note 22

24 See note 12

25 *Disability Briefing*, (Source: Labour Force Survey Spring 2001, Great Britain), Disability Rights Commission, December 2001

26 See Chapter 2, Analytical Services Division, Department for Work and Pensions, 2002

27 Analytical Services Division, *Work and Pension Statistics 2001*, Department for Work and Pensions, 2001

28 'Incapacity Benefit: new rules on work', *Working Brief*, Issue 134, Centre for Economic and Social Inclusion, May 2002

29 See note 25

30 See note 22

31 *Statistical First Release*, Department for Work and Pensions, February 2002

32 See note 12

33 See note 12

34 P Bivand, 'Ethnic Minorities and the Labour Market', *Working Brief*, Issue 132, Centre for Economic and Social Inclusion, March 2002

35 *The National Minimum Wage, Making a Difference: the next steps*, third report of the Low Pay Commission, Vol 2, Low Pay Commission, 2001

36 See note 34

37 *Ethnic Minorities and the Labour Market: interim analytical report*, Cabinet, Performance and Innovation Unit, 2002

38 *Social Justice, Annual Report 2001* (Annex: Indicators of Progress), Scottish Executive, 2002

39 *Statistical First Release*, Department for Work and Pensions, February 2002

40 *Scottish Social Statistics 2001*, Scottish Executive, 2001

41 *Disadvantage and Discrimination in Britain Today: the facts*, Commission for Racial Equality, 2001

42 K Chahal and L Julienne, *'We can't all be White' Racist Victimisation in the UK*, Joseph Rowntree Foundation, 1999

43 *Older People in the United Kingdom: basic facts*, Age Concern, 2001

44 Analytical Services Division, *Pensioners' Incomes Series 1999/00*, Department for Work and Pensions, 2001

45 M Howard, A Garnham, G Fimister and J Veit-Wilson, *Poverty: the facts*, Child Poverty Action Group, 2001

46 See note 44

47 See note 6

48 See note 44

49 *Family Spending: report on the 1999-2000 Family Spending Expenditure Survey*, Office for National Statistics, 2000

50 M Carrado and L Vinter, *Attitudes Towards Income in Retirement for Age Concern*, MORI, 2002

51 M Rahman, G Palmer and P Kenway, *Monitoring Poverty and Social Exclusion 2001*, New Policy Institute, Joseph Rowntree Foundation, 2001

52 *Labour Force Survey*, Office for National Statistics, 2002

53 See note 51

54 *The National Minimum Wage: making a difference*, Third Report of the Low Pay Commission, 2001

55 *New Deal for Unemployed People in Scotland: statistics to end January 2002*, Scottish Executive Publications Online, 22 April 2002

56 *The New Deal for Young People,* Report by Comptroller and Auditor General, HC 639 Session 2001-2002, The Stationery Office, 28 February 2002

57 'New Deal Sanctions', *Working Brief*, Issue 132, Centre for Economic and Social Inclusion, March 2002

58 L Britton, 'Sanctions and the Hard to Help', *Working Brief*, Issue 130, Centre for Economic and Social Inclusion, January 2002

59 See note 51

60 See note 38

61 *New Deal for Unemployed People in Scotland: statistics to end January 2002*, Table A6: qualifications on entry for those joining New Deal 18–24 to end

January 2002, Scottish Executive Publications Online, 22 April 2002

62 L Philip, 'Assessing Rural and Urban Poverty', in *Poverty in Scotland: information for a change*, Conference Report, Scottish Poverty Information Unit, 1998

63 *Employment, Housing and Poverty in Rural Areas*, Research Note, prepared for the Rural Affairs Committee, Information Centre, The Scottish Parliament, August 1999

64 *The Scottish Household Survey*, Bulletin 6, Scottish Executive, 2001

65 Gibb, Kearnes, Keoghan, Makay, and Turok, *Revising the Scottish Area Deprivation Index*, Central Research Unit, Scottish Office, 1998

66 See note 64

# Five
# Living with poverty

Poverty means diminished life chances. For some it may entail going without essentials such as sufficient food, adequate housing, heating and enough clothing. For many it will also mean having to live without access to the services or social activities that others consider normal; in effect being excluded from taking part in society. This section briefly covers some aspects of life that are affected by poverty: housing and homelessness, fuel poverty, debt and health.

## Housing and homelessness

In Scotland generally, like the rest of Great Britain, there has been a steady increase in owner-occupation and a decrease in renting from public sector bodies. The effect is uneven though, as urban areas retain considerably higher proportions of local authority rented housing than the rest of the country. Table 5.1 shows the number and percentage of owner-occupied and public sector housing in Scotland in 1992, 1996 and 2000.

The number of owner-occupied dwellings increased by 25 per cent between 1992 and 2000 and those rented from public authorities decreased by 29 per cent in the same period.

Table 5.1

**Owner-occupied and public authority rented dwellings, 1992, 1996 and 2000, Scotland**

|  | 1992 | 1996 | 2000 |
|---|---|---|---|
| Estimated stock of dwellings at 31 December (000s) | 2,175 | 2,248 | 2,325 |
| % owner-occupied | 54.1 | 59.0 | 63.1 |
| % rented from public authorities | 36.0 | 29.7 | 24.0 |

Source: Scottish Executive, *Statistical Bulletin: Housing Series*, HSG/2001/6, 2001, Table 1

Table 5.2

**Percentage of household types (row percentages), by household tenure, 1999/2000, Scotland**

|  | Owned outright | Buying with loan/ mortgage | Renting from public authority | Renting from private landlord | Other |
|---|---|---|---|---|---|
| Single adult | 12 | 36 | 38 | 12 | 2 |
| Single parent | 4 | 19 | 69 | 7 | 1 |
| Small family | 6 | 69 | 20 | 3 | 1 |
| Large family | 8 | 60 | 26 | 4 | 2 |
| Single pensioner | 41 | 6 | 48 | 3 | 2 |
| All | 24 | 38 | 31 | 5 | 2 |

Source: Scottish Executive, *Scottish Household Survey 1999/00*, Annual Report Vol 3, 2001, Table 2.6

Table 5.2 shows the percentage of household types by tenure in Scotland in 1999/2000.

Owner occupation is highest among small (69 per cent) and large families (60 per cent). Around a quarter of large families and a fifth of small families are public sector tenants.

Over two-thirds of lone parents (69 per cent) are public sector tenants, 23 per cent are owner-occupiers.

The change in tenure pattern is important; increasingly, local authority housing is becoming a residual sector for people with low incomes, many of whom are in receipt of state benefits. Many owner-occupiers also experience poverty, particularly older people whose incomes have fallen since retirement, and who can no longer afford adequate heating or essential repairs. Furthermore, for many people from minority ethnic communities, buying a house has been the only way of avoiding discrimination in housing allocation, even though they have had inadequate resources. Low-income households are more likely to live in poor housing, which they often cannot afford to repair. Poor housing can cause ill health. A report by the Scottish Executive in 1999 found that houses with cold, damp and mouldy conditions pose a great risk to health, and the prevalence of illness increased with the level of dampness.[1]

## Homelessness

There has been a steady growth in homelessness over the last twenty years. A recent study found that the level of homelessness is affected by wider structural factors, in particular unemployment, housing affordability and de-institutionalisation. The report concluded:

> 'While behavioural factors may be important in explaining individual cases of homelessness, the analysis indicates that structural trends do affect the aggregate level of homelessness.' [2]

The Scottish Executive collects figures on the number of households that apply to local authorities as homeless. But there are many who never appear in local authority records. The most under-recorded group is single homeless people, few of whom the councils have a legal duty to house.

Table 5.3 shows the number of homeless applications made to local authorities between 1996/97 and 2000/01.

Table 5.3

**Number of applications to local authorities made by households under the homeless persons legislation; 1996/97-2000/01, Scotland**

|  | Number of applications |
|---|---|
| 1996/97 | 40,989 |
| 1997/98 | 43,135 |
| 1998/99 | 45,723 |
| 1999/2000 | 46,023 |
| 2000/01 | 45,172 |

Source: Scottish Executive, *Statistical Bulletin: Housing Series*, HSG/2001/6, 2001, Table 24

From 1996/97 to 2000/01 there was an increase of 10.2 per cent in the number of applications made. There was a slight decrease in applications between 1999/2000 and 2000/01.

Table 5.4

**Number and percentage of households and dependent children in temporary accommodation, end June 2001, Scotland**

|  | All households | | Households with dependent children | | Total number of dependent children | |
|---|---|---|---|---|---|---|
|  | No. | % | No. | % | No. | % |
| Local authority dwelling | 2,143 | 53 | 1,167 | 83 | 2,206 | 84 |
| Hostel | 1,309 | 33 | 101 | 7 | 188 | 7 |
| Bed and breakfast | 483 | 12 | 88 | 6 | 149 | 6 |
| Other | 71 | 2 | 50 | 4 | 82 | 3 |
| **Totals** | **4,006** | **100** | **1,406** | **100** | **2,625** | **100** |

Source: Scottish Executive, *Statistical Bulletin: Housing Series*, HSG/2001/6, 2001, Table 26

Note: The category 'other' includes mainly housing associations and private landlords.

The majority of households with children (83 per cent) were housed in local authority housing. There were 337 children living in hostels or bed and breakfast accommodation in June 2001 in Scotland. When all households in temporary accommodation are considered, just over half were in local authority housing, around a third were in hostels.

# Fuel poverty

Fuel poverty occurs when households cannot keep warm at a reasonable cost:

'It is the combination of low income, energy prices and poor energy efficiency that results in fuel poverty. The fuel-poor tend to have the lowest mean income, but also the highest mean required fuel costs.'[3]

It has been estimated that around three in ten households in Scotland experience, or are at risk of, fuel poverty.[4] Living with fuel poverty has serious consequences for health: these include hypothermia, asthma, respiratory diseases and higher mortality rates in winter. In addition, spending on heating often involves making cuts in other areas such as food or social and leisure activities, which also impact on health and quality of life.[5]

## Debt

Living on a low income brings with it the threat of falling into debt. Low-income households most frequently fall behind on payments of basic household bills, such as rent, electricity, gas, water and council tax, as opposed to the consumer credit arrears accumulated by better-off debtors. These kinds of debts tend to incur the harshest of sanctions in terms of repossession, disconnection, fines and even imprisonment. Research shows that most people are ashamed of being in debt, and that those who owe money on major household bills acknowledge their debt and therefore their obligations to creditors:

> 'Their situation is therefore one of 'can't pay' rather than 'won't pay'.'[6]

Some claimants live below income support level because they have their benefit reduced by deductions for debt. Benefit deductions are made for social fund loans, overpayments, debts or fines. In Great Britain (November 2001) around 1.22 million (31 per cent) of income support claimants had one or more deductions from their weekly benefit.[7] The largest groups paying deductions were lone parents, disabled people and pensioners. The most common type of deduction was for repayment of a social fund loan. The majority of social fund loans are for essential household equipment such as beds, cookers and washing machines. There has been an increase in the number of deductions for social fund loans: from 582,000 in November in 1997 to 794,000 in November 2001.[8]

## Health

The relationship between health and income is complex but fundamental. Household income is the largest determinant of living standards, influencing the type of house a family can afford, and access to space, leisure, food, heating and clothing, all of which have a direct impact on both physical and mental well-being. Sir Donald Acheson's independent inquiry in

1998, based on data covering England and Wales, found that health inequalities had increased since the 1970s. The Acheson report concluded that the rise in poverty and income inequality over the last two decades is likely to have made a substantial contribution to the widening gap in health status across socio-economic groups.[9] Research in Scotland reveals similar trends.

The measure used in the figures below is a Standardised Mortality Ratio (SMR), which adjusts for differences in the age and sex composition of groups.

Mortality rates for men and women in deprivation category seven are higher than all other categories. In all categories, male mortality rates are higher than female rates.

Figure 5.1

**Mortality age-standardised rates (rates per 100,000 population), by deprivation category and gender, 2000 Scotland**

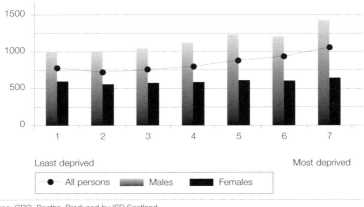

Source: GRO, Deaths. Produced by ISD Scotland

Figure 5.2

**Mortality age-standardised rates for selected causes, by deprivation category, 2000, Scotland**

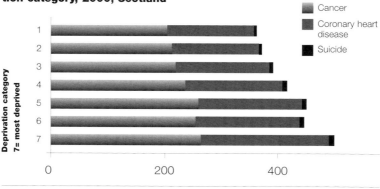

Source: GRO, Deaths. Produced by ISD Scotland

Mortality rates for all the selected causes above are higher for category seven.

For suicide the mortality rates for males in deprivation category seven are 4.1 times higher than rates for males in category one.

## Notes

1   D Wilkinson, *Poor Housing and Ill Heath: a summary of research evidence*, Central Research Unit, The Scottish Office, 1999

2   P Kemp, D MacKay and E Lynch, *Structural Trends and Homelessness: a quantitative analysis*, Development Department Research Programme, Research Report No 124, Central Research Unit, Scottish Executive

3   *The Scottish Fuel Poverty Statement – Consultative Draft*, Scottish Executive, March 2002

4   See note 3

5   *The Impact of Fuel Poverty and Housing Conditions on Scotland's Health: a review of the available literature*, Energy Action Scotland, 1998

6   E Kempson, *Life on Low Income*, Joseph Rowntree Foundation, 1996

7   Information Centre, Analytical Services Division, *Income Support Quarterly Statistical Enquiry*, Department for Work and Pensions, November 2001

8   See note 7

9   D Acheson, *Independent Inquiry into Inequalities in Health*, The Stationery Office, 1998

# Section three
# **People, places, politics**

# Six

# Child poverty in Scotland

*Danny Phillips, Child Poverty Action Group in Scotland*

'Poverty is not simply an economic issue where children are concerned. For children, poverty often means physical, emotional or intellectual impairment, which can add up to a lifetime of lost opportunity – and a legacy of poverty for succeeding generations … [The] eradication of the worst manifestations of poverty is not only a moral imperative. It is a practical and affordable possibility – and it starts with investing in children.'(Carol Bellamy, Executive Director, UNICEF)

In Scotland children are the group most likely to be poor and most likely to remain poor for a long period of time, and younger children are more likely to live in poverty than older children. Children *become* poor because of social and economic reasons such as: unemployment; changing family circumstances, for instance divorce; or because of additional costs, for example as a result of the illness of a family member. But children are poor because they and their family lack resources: access to services, markets and, fundamentally, income.

In March 1999, Tony Blair pledged to end child poverty within a generation. The Scottish Executive followed quickly, noting in its annual report, *Social Justice: a Scotland where everyone matters* (November 1999) 'above all we wish to make child poverty a thing of the past within a generation'. Soon after, in the Public Service Agreement (PSA), the Treasury set targets to *end* child poverty by 2019, half it by 2010 and quarter it by 2004. The Executive and Department for Work and Pensions announced further targets and that progress would be monitored in annual reports.[1]

The importance of these ambitions should not be underestimated. Governments have been concerned with poverty in the past – Mrs Thatcher famously stood on a derelict industrial site in Teesside promising to bring renewed prosperity to Britain's run-down urban areas by promoting private property and enterprise and in the 1960s the Wilson

Government was concerned with pockets of poverty and experimented with educational priority areas.[2] But no government in the UK has pledged to *eradicate* child poverty before. We may argue about definitions, policies, targets, measurements and timescales but the pledge to end child poverty should receive our unfaltering support.

## Progress so far by the Scottish Executive and UK government

The Treasury stated: 'Tax and benefit reforms announced in this parliament [19972001] will lift over 1.2 million children out of relative poverty.' However, official figures released on 11 April 2002 show child poverty fell, in the UK, by 0.5 million from 4.4 million in 1996/97 to 3.9 million 2000/01.[3] Child poverty in Scotland fell from 34 per cent in 1996/97 to 30 per cent in 2000/01. Progress, albeit slow, is in the right direction but there is a serious danger of not attaining the next PSA targets. We should not overlook the welcome fact that at least 500,000 children across the UK were lifted out of poverty between 1997 and 2001, but child poverty is still extremely high by post-war standards and vulnerable to the state of the economy. In Scotland, a relatively small country of one million children, over 300,000 children live in poverty.

There are a number of reasons why decreases in child poverty have been comparatively modest, some of which have to do with statistical and technical problems involved in the shape, form and level of thresholds and measurements. The Government is currently consulting on the development of new child poverty measures. Moreover, because the *Households Below Average Income* (HBAI) data is at least a year behind, the effects of government polices may not have shown up. For example, the relatively significant increases in income support child allowances, introduced in 1999, can be seen in the HBAI data on child poverty in 2000/01, but the impact of working families' tax credit (WFTC), introduced in October 2000, will only be fully seen in the next set of HBAI figures. The latest HBAI figures produced analyse child poverty in 2000/01 and therefore up to 150,000 children may not have been included in these figures.[4]

There are also a number of policy issues that have not helped the government strategy to eradicate child poverty. Child poverty is, fundamentally, being tackled through WFTC, child benefit and income support. While child benefit is a very successful benefit, income support and tax credits are less so. Due to seemingly intractable take-up problems with means-testing, only 62 per cent of children in families with an entitlement actually receive WFTC[5] and only 90 per cent receive income support.

## Working families tax credit

WFTC, which came into effect in April 2000, is a benefit for working families. Its aim is to reinforce the impact of the minimum wage, target low-income families, reduce poverty and strengthen the family unit. Since April 2001 it has been paid through the wage packet in order to deal with some of the difficulties associated with means-testing, such as stigma and poor take-up.

In Scotland, the overall number of awards, the level of awards, and the take-up of WFTC among those entitled showed improvements over the old family credit system. In August 1999 there were 81,900 family credit awards and in February 2001 there were 114,200 WFTC awards, amounting to 9 per cent of the Scottish population.[6] Take-up of WFTC also increased to between 73–77 per cent (family credit was 66–70 per cent), as did amounts payable; the average WFTC award in Scotland increased by £16.85 in February 2001 over family credit in August 1999.

However, take-up fell well short of government targets causing concern about WFTC's impact on child poverty. The main barrier for low-income families moving into work is the concern about how they will meet their housing costs and, crucially, WFTC still counts as income for housing and council tax benefits. Loss of passport benefits like free school meals, prescriptions, school uniform grants and milk tokens means an increase in wages could amount to a real decrease in family disposable income. Short-term, insecure and low-paid work still proves too risky for many families.

## New child tax credit

In order to overcome some of the difficulties of WFTC and to ensure continuous support for children and their families WFTC is to be replaced by the integrated child tax credit (CTC). It will be implemented in 2003. This is a means-tested benefit for low-income families with children, whether in or out of work, and brings together in one payment existing means-tested support for children. Its aims are to make work pay and tackle child poverty in workless households through a single simplified payment for children. In April 2003, WFTC, children's tax credit, disabled person's tax credit, income support/job seeker's allowance, child, and family and child dependant allowances for other benefits will be abolished.

There is a consensus that CTC can make a significant reduction in child poverty: it is a potential means of securing additional resources for low-income families. However, in order to do so, it must be set at an adequate level. The End Child Poverty Coalition (UK) is calling on the Government to set the new CTC and child benefit at £62.60 for the first child and £47 for the second child.[7] It argues this will lift a further one million children out of poverty in the UK, approximately 100,000 in Scotland.[8]

While many of the harsher aspects of means-testing are not part of CTC – for instance there are no capital rules, and awards are not effected by significant increases in income – there is concern that assessments will be based on an estimate of a family's income for the whole tax year. This will reduce certainty about how much a family will receive from year to year, and there is the possibility of large over or under-payments through poor assessments. We await decisions on passported benefits.

## Job retention and advancement

A key aspect of the Government's anti-poverty policy is to enable people to find work and to ensure work pays. It was hoped that people 'would move up the employment ladder, seeing their earnings increase as they do so'.[9] However, there is evidence that while there may be an increase in families in work, they do not tend to progress to more skilled or better paid employment. About half those who leave claimant unemployment for work 'sign-on' again within a year and one in seven are unemployed by the thirteenth week.[10]

In-work policies, so far, have tended to assist families who already have one parent in work and have been less effective in helping workless families and the long-term unemployed. Policies therefore have had less effect in areas with high concentrations of multiple deprivation, found in Britain's poorest constituencies such as Shettleston, Springburn, and Maryhill in Glasgow.[11]

## 'Hearts and minds'

Overall, the Government has completed the easiest job first. Those children nearest the poverty line have been pushed above it. Those families who can access work, or who already had work, have benefited from the more generous WFTC (over family credit), from increased take-up of WFTC over family credit[12] and from the introduction of the minimum wage.

> 'Some good [has been done] by stealth: the rest will need taxpayers' informed consent for sizeable redistribution over the next twenty years [we need to] create a campaign to spark the public imagination.'[13]

Crucial to ending child poverty in Scotland is the need to build a social consensus that children are a collective investment and the responsibility of us all, rather than a private cost and the sole responsibility of their parents.

This is why people in Scotland must be convinced that the eradication of child poverty is not only economically and socially imperative – increasing productivity, fighting crime, reducing ill health and rising health service costs – but that it is also a *moral* imperative. It is simply unacceptable in a rich nation such as Scotland that children should go without basic necessities or be socially excluded from mainstream Scottish society. Hearts and minds must be won. It is the task of campaigners, trade unions, churches, charities, businesses and all political parties to ensure that 'a generation' is the maximum time we must wait for an end to child poverty. Only when child poverty is at an end can Scotland can call itself a modern country.

### Notes

1   Annual government monitors are *Opportunity for All*, Department for Work and Pensions and the *Annual Social Justice Report*, Scottish Executive

2   P Alcock, 'Neighbourhood Renewal' in G Fimister, *An End In Sight? Tackling child poverty in the UK*, Child Poverty Action Group, 2001

3   *The Government's Child Poverty Target: how much progress has been made?* Commentary 87, Institute for Fiscal Studies, 2002

4   See note 3

5   M Brewer, 'Personal Tax Reforms', in Dilnot *et al*, *The IFS Green Budget 2002*, Institute for Fiscal Studies, 2002

6   *Working Families' Tax Credit*, Briefing Sheet No 16, Scottish Poverty Information Unit, November 2001

7  *End Child Poverty: tax and benefits briefing paper*, End Child Poverty Campaign

8  Figure based on calculation that approximately 10 per cent of the population live in Scotland.

9  HM Treasury, *Equipping Britain for our Long-term Future*, Financial Statement and Budget Report, HC paper 346-I, The Stationery Office, 1997

10  See 'Work after Welfare', *Benefits: a journal of social security research, policy and practice*, No 34, Vol 10, Issue 2, June 2002

11  J Seymour, *Poverty in Plenty: a human development report for the UK*, UNED-UK, 2000

12  Inland Revenue, *Working Families' Tax Credits*, Quarterly Enquiry, taken from SPIU Briefing Sheet 16, November 2001

13  P Toynbee, *The Guardian*, 21 December 2001

# Seven
# Social policy and family poverty
*Gill Scott, Scottish Poverty Information Unit*

It is a major and perhaps impossible task to map out and make sense of the development of all the policies that have had an impact on family life since 1997. There is no doubt, however, that a significant and very positive feature of both the Westminster-based New Labour Government, and the new Scottish Executive has been a growing and explicit concern with family in social policy. We have seen, for example, a first-ever consultation paper on family policy, *Supporting Families* (1998), largely mirrored in the Scottish Office paper *Helping the Family in Scotland* (1999). The Government has taken up a campaign on the work-family balance through new legislation and policies on parental leave. Ending family and child poverty has become a major aim of family policies of government at UK and Scottish level.

## Policy direction

A variety of policies have been pursued as a result. Chancellor Brown, for example, has made support for families with children one of the foundations on which the tax and benefits system is built. The Scottish Executive's social justice strategy includes a range of services for families in deprived areas under the Sure Start Scotland programme and Healthy Living Centre initiatives, as well as Parentline policies.[1]

Two directions can be identified in such policies. On the one hand there are policies designed to support and direct the role of families as the basis of a more moral, dutiful and cohesive community.[2] Suggestions of reductions in child benefit for 'socially irresponsible' parents was a controlling aspect of such a view.[3] Sure Start and Parentline represent more supportive approaches. Paid work as the only permanent way out of poverty for families is, however, the more powerful logic driving the majority of policies with significant impact on family poverty. The New Deals for lone parents and partners of the unemployed, working families' tax credit (WFTC) and its successor the integrated child tax credit (CTC), minimum wage legislation and large elements of the national childcare strategy are designed primarily to make it easier for parents to increase family resources through work.

## Effects of policy

There can be little doubt that the strategy has had some positive effects. Since Spring 1997, unemployment has dropped by 25 per cent overall, and long-term male unemployment by 48 per cent. The Scottish Executive reports that employment opportunities are increasing, with around 75,000 new jobs created since Spring 1997, and employment rates for disadvantaged groups including lone parents are also increasing.[4] The impact of this for low-income households with children is significant: the percentage of children in Scotland living in workless households has fallen since 1997. However, it should be remembered that labour market entry may not be positive for every family. A recent study of poverty dynamics in the UK showed the relative importance of the labour market providing a route out of poverty. Movement into the labour force accounted for 48 per cent of exits from poverty.[5] However, for 30 per cent of households where a member re-entered the labour market there was no benefit. Evidence from America, where 'welfare to work' has been established for longer, suggests that increased parental involvement in work is successful in removing children from poverty in only 50 per cent of cases.[6]

Looking to specific elements of family policy introduced since 1997 some writers argue that, while successes can be found, fundamental flaws in the fiscal policies limit the impact on family poverty. WFTC, for example, addressed some of the issues faced by lone mothers participating in the labour market. Increased premiums for children and increased childcare credits have meant that work does indeed pay for some women. However, it could be said that WFTC represents a reworking of the male breadwinner model and when non-employed female partners of male WFTC recipients take paid employment it often results in a loss of real income due to losses in housing and council tax benefits. Coupled with the increased costs of travel to work, and funding of 30 per cent of child-care costs, paid work may not effectively raise family income, and perhaps even more significantly, it may add extra strains on money management schemes within households. The payment of WFTC through the wage packet can mean male breadwinners have the potential to retain a larger proportion of their earnings and women and children can lose out. Consequently, gender income inequalities *within* families can be reinforced by the payment of WFTC through the wage packet and to the main earner.[7]

Further criticisms are directed at what the policy ignores, rather than what it underestimates. Work-life balance has been part of the rhetoric of anti-poverty policy for families. However, there is little hard evidence that strategies that could encourage employers to consider implementing such policies for low-paid workers as well as the more highly paid are being addressed seriously. Nor do fiscal or childcare policies that allow families real choices in balancing family and work appear to have been developed. Indeed the potential contradiction between encouraging parents, particu-larly lone parents, into the workforce and emphasising parenting responsi-bilities is largely fudged. To some extent this is because the role of citizen as worker rather than citizen as carer drives the thinking of welfare reform, and the value of caring work done by parents (and for parents at later ages) is simply not recognised.

## Childcare

The lack of recognition of the hard, skilled and time-consuming work of childcare is also evident in the problems that beset the implementation of the national childcare strategy. The recognition of under-provision of child-care, plus the focus by the Labour Government since 1997 on reducing child poverty and promoting area regeneration has led to the adoption of childcare as a key element in anti-poverty policy. In July 2001, for exam-ple, the Government announced the approval of plans for 45,000 new childcare places in 900 neighbourhood nursery centres, together with an addition of £40 million for capital spending on early years education in dis-advantaged areas.[8]

The development of adequate, affordable childcare has been pro-moted to enable low-paid mothers, particularly lone mothers, to go into paid work but it has also been seen as a means to create employment in childcare jobs for women in areas of deprivation. Recent research in

Scotland, however, suggests that childcare provision remains patchily provided, insecurely funded and unevenly developed. Over 90 per cent of all daycare provision is *funded to some extent* by charges or fund raising by parents. Local authority funding is received by less than 30 per cent of service providers.[9] Despite changes in government policy, childcare still seems to be a service for which parents are financially responsible. There is little private sector involvement in providing childcare services to areas of deprivation and the infrastructure necessary to further current government policies is lacking. Indeed, tensions between economic and social agendas on childcare are clearly evident in the childcare partnerships that have been set up across the country. Childcare work, moreover, appears to be insecure, largely part time and generally low paid. 'Welfare to work' policies that are developed in a vacuum, without attention to the low-skilled jobs that are at times created by them can bring particular problems for women in low-income households trying to balance childcare and sustainable employment.[10]

There is, perhaps even more worryingly, evidence from international studies of family policy and poverty reduction that needs to be considered. Throughout Europe family poverty is lowest where families are supported in gaining income from the state *and* from the labour market, *and* where the 'social wage' is high, especially in respect of childcare provision.[11] The European emphasis on reconciling care for children with paid employment through widespread public childcare provision and parental leave has still to be fully addressed in the UK. The result is that poverty remains a problem for families inside and outside the labour market. For those with major caring roles and limited access to the labour market, particularly lone parents, social security, public housing and community assets have changed insufficiently to remove the risk of poverty. For those who enter the labour market in low-paid jobs (that are a result of labour market policies more concerned with increases in the number of jobs rather than the type of jobs that are emerging), the social wage in the form of child benefit, childcare or housing is once again insufficient to ensure that their children are protected from the risk of poverty.

## The way ahead

With such problems, what is the way ahead for policies designed to reduce family poverty? The challenges are ones that the Scottish

Executive must face, but they are also fundamentally linked to the fiscal and social security issues of Westminster. They include:

- paying attention to structural change in employment to ensure that the most vulnerable families are not faced with insecure work when members move into work;
- improved housing access for households with children;
- childcare based on children's needs;
- some re-allocation of resources for the bottom 10-20 per cent of families. There is a problem of growing inequality, not just poverty.

Families in bad housing, with sub-standard schools, few community facilities and poor transport will continue to find it difficult to plan for their own and their children's future if the major policy approach on offer drives them to combine poor work with household and community assets continually at risk. As Folbre argues, members of a society share the benefits of children brought up well.[12] When other services have a 'public good' aspect, the state steps in to socialise the costs. Is it not time child-rearing was treated in the same way?

## Notes

1  F Wasoff and I Dey, *Family Policy*, Gildredge Press, 2000

2  S Driver and L Martell, 'New Labour, Work and the Family', *Social Policy and Administration*, Vol 36, No 1, 2002, pp46-61

3  G Hinscliff, 'Parents Face Benefits Axe Over Unruly Children', *The Guardian*, 28 April 2002

4  *Social Justice Report 2001*, Scottish Executive, 2001

5  S P Jenkins and J Rigg, *The Dynamics of Poverty in Britain*, Department for Work and Pensions, Research Report No157, 2001

6  Child Trends Research Brief, *Working Poor Families with Children*, 1999

7  A Gray, 'Making Work Pay: devising the best strategy for lone parents in Britain', *Journal of Social Policy*, Vol 30, 2001

8  Department for Education and Skills, Press Release, 24 July 2001

9  *Social Work Daycare Services Statistical Note*, Scottish Office, November 1999

10 G Scott, J Campbell and U Brown, 'The Contribution of Childcare to Local Employment: poor work or work for the poor?', *Local Economy*, 2001

11 K Christopher et al, 'Gender Inequality in Poverty in Affluent Nations: the role of single motherhood and the state', in K Vleminckx and T Sweeting, *Child Wellbeing, Child Poverty and Child Policy in Modern Nations*, Policy Press, 2001

12 N Folbre, 'Children as Public Goods', *American Economic Review*, Vol 84, No 2, 1984, pp86-90

# Eight
# Local areas and regeneration
*Gerry Mooney, Open University*

## New Labour and divided Britain

'We all know the problems of our poorest neighbourhoods – decaying housing, unemployment, street crime and drugs. People, who can, move out.
Nightmare neighbours move in. Shops, banks and other vital services close.
Over the last two decades the gap between these 'worst estates' and the
rest of the country has grown. It has left us with a situation that no civilised
society should tolerate... It shames us as a nation, it wastes lives and we
all have to pay the costs of dependency and social division.' (Tony Blair,
1998) [1]

On coming to power in 1997 the New Labour Government faced a land-
scape that was increasingly divided. There was considerable evidence
that pointed to deepening inequalities between different parts of the country both contributing to and reflecting the increasing *social polarisation*
between rich and poor.[2] These trends were manifested in a growing cat-
alogue of data that highlighted marked inequalities in health, education,
income and a host of other aspects of daily living between different groups
in different areas. Life chances, it was confirmed, were both directly and
indirectly affected by where we live.[3] The existence of such marked *and
growing* inequalities between localities has led to a revival of interest in
poor neighbourhoods and tackling the problems of such localities is central to the Government's social inclusion and social policy agenda.

## A geographically divided Scotland?

Disadvantage and inequality are to be found the length and breadth of
Scotland. But 'divided Scotland' is not simply and solely on the grounds
of poverty. We must not forget that Scotland remains a comparatively rich

society and in this respect geographically related divisions of wealth continue to be a significant feature of modern society. The authors of a Scottish Council Foundation report argued that:

> 'Scotland like the rest of Britain is becoming more unequal in life and death. Inequalities in income, earnings and wealth continue to grow.'[4]

While policy makers, politicians and academics strive to highlight geographical concentrations of poverty, the fact that some of the richest localities (for example, Bearsden, Milngavie and East Renfrewshire/ Eastwood) lie adjacent to some of the poorest (Glasgow's peripheral estates) often passes with little comment.[5] In this process the relationships between poverty and wealth are neglected.

## Area-based policies in Scotland

> 'Too often in the past strategies to tackle poverty and injustice in Scotland have been more about places than they have been about people… Our communities need to be supported to be able to take more ownership of their own destinies. Too many Scottish communities and neighbourhoods are isolated and disadvantaged, or in danger of becoming so. We believe that every community matters and we need to work together with them to plan for a more inclusive future.' (Scottish Office, 1999)[6]

From the late 1990s the Scottish Office and subsequently the Scottish Parliament have placed the problems of socially excluded communities at the centre of its social justice and social inclusion strategies.[7] 'Reducing inequalities between areas', 'reviving and empowering communities' and 'tackling crime and disorder' are central goals in this overall approach. There has been a plethora of initiatives, including the Better Neighbourhood Services Fund designed to improve service delivery and promote participation in disadvantaged areas. The ongoing review of Scottish cities policy, initiated by former First Minister Henry McLeish, promises to deliver new policies for Scotland's cities and the social inclusion partnerships (SIPs). Commencing in May 1998, the SIPs arguably represent the most important area-based regeneration programme in Scotland today.

## Social inclusion partnerships

SIPs are an extension of the urban programmes of the 1980s and 1990s. They are designed to tackle physical, economic and social decay in areas of high unemployment, low income, poor health and educational under-achievement, and were announced as policy in 1998. There are 48 SIPs in Scotland, 14 of them are thematic. The SIPs, like past initiatives such as 'New Life for Urban Scotland' launched in 1988 and the 'priority part-nership areas' (1996), focus on and stress *'partnership'* and *'community involvement'*. There is a continuing emphasis on the management of serv-ice delivery and on the co-ordination of government programmes in dis-advantaged areas. However, the key difference is that the focus is no longer simply on 'bricks and mortar' or physical regeneration, but crucial-ly involves *social regeneration*. Thus, strategies to promote employability, inclusion and to create *sustainable* communities rich in *social capital* are to the fore with an emphasis on educational initiatives, training and employability.

Core funding of £179 million over three years was committed to the policy and a further £1 million to support the development of community participation skills for residents, partnership officers and agencies. The focus on improving the social capacity of poorer areas through a multitude of local initiatives is also expected to have a particularly significant effect on the potential of residents to enter employment and thus put them on a route out of poverty. However, there have been a number of criticisms of SIP policy including:

- serious doubts about area-based partnerships as a way to address the underlying employment base in the areas;[8]
- as with previous area-based initiatives, the fact that the extent of com-munity participation that has actually been developed may be minimal;[9]
- the limited extent of women's involvement in, and benefit from, part-nerships;[10] *and*
- the limited potential of the partnership approach in reducing inequali-ties between areas of declining and developing economic change, namely Glasgow and Edinburgh in Scotland.[11]

One strand of SIP policy is their focus on tackling crime and promoting youth justice and community safety schemes. While government policy *does* talk to real fears and concerns, none-the-less it is important to retain critical awareness of the claims being made and the ways in which disadvantaged areas are being constructed and understood.

## Concluding comments

New Labour's locality or community-based policies today reflect a particular understanding of the nature of social problems. While these are still seen as area-based there is a growing recognition that such problems also transcend particular localities as reflected in the creation of thematic SIPs. While this is a step forward, none-the-less there is a discernible tendency to construct those housing schemes and other areas targeted by spatially-based policy as in some senses pathological, outside or at least marginal to what is unproblematically defined as mainstream society.

> 'While most areas have benefited from rising living standards, the poorest neighbourhoods have tended to become more rundown, more prone to crime, and more cut off from the labour market. The national picture conceals pockets of intense deprivation where the problems of unemployment and crime are acute and tangled up with poor health, housing, and education. They have become no go areas for some and no exit zones for others.'[12]

There is an obvious danger that problems are constructed as lying within discrete neighbourhoods. Clearly there is a focus on the problems of poor, disadvantaged or socially excluded locales. But what is neglected are the widening and deepening inequalities between different localities within Scotland. It is also important to acknowledge that government social, economic and fiscal policy in recent decades has contributed to concentrate poverty and disadvantage. The lack of investment in social infrastructure such as housing, education and community facilities was compounded in the eighties and nineties by the withdrawal of private sector services in many localities. It is a trend that continues and is becoming more significant, as the private sector plays an ever more important role in social provision.

Finally, while focusing on poor localities is vital, we must not forget that the most significant processes that contribute to geographically based disadvantage are to be found in the wider structures of inequality and social division within contemporary Scottish society. Unless inequalities of wealth and income are tackled there will be a tendency to portray disadvantaged localities as in some way to blame for their own misfortune, while the issues of inequality remain neglected.

## Notes

1   Foreword, in Social Exclusion Unit, *Bringing Britain Together: a national strategy for neighbourhood renewal*, HMSO, 1998

2   See Chapter 8 in M Howard, A Garnham, G Fimister and J Veit-Wilson, *Poverty: the facts*, Child Poverty Action Group, 2001

3   For example, M Mackintosh and G Mooney, 'Identity, Inequality and Social Class', in K Woodward (ed), *Questioning Identity: gender, class, nation*, Routledge/The Open University, 2000; and L Janes and G Mooney, 'Place, Lifestyle and Social Divisions', in P Braham and L Janes (eds), *Social Differences and Divisions*, Blackwell/The Open University, 2002

4   L Boyes, M Davies, D Elrick, G Leicester, A Lyon and J McCormick, *Out of the Ordinary*, Scottish Council Foundation, 2001, p13

5   For example, A E Green, *The Geography of Poverty and Wealth*, University of Warwick Institute for Employment Research, 1994; and CACI, Paycheck 1999, CACI plc, 2001

6   Scottish Office, *Social Justice: a Scotland where everyone matters*, Scottish Office, 1999, p7

7   For example, Scottish Office, *Social Inclusion: opening the door to a better Scotland*, Scottish Office, 1999; Scottish Office, *Social Justice: a Scotland where everyone matters*, Scottish Office, 1999; and Scottish Executive, *Social Justice: a Scotland where everyone matters: Annual Report 2001*, Scottish Executive, 2001

8   D Webster, 'Targeted Local Jobs: the missing element in New Labour's 'social inclusion' policy', *New Economy*, December 1999

9   A Hastings, A McArthur and A McGregor, *Less than Equal? Community organisations and estate regeneration partnerships*, The Policy Press/Joseph Rowntree Foundation, 1996

10  G Scott, U Brown, G Long and J Mackenzie, *Women's Issues in Local Partnership Working*, Central Research Unit, Scottish Executive, 2000

11  I Turok and N Edge, *The Jobs Gap in Britain's Cities: employment loss and the labour market consequence*, The Policy Press, 2000

12  Social Exclusion Unit, *Bringing Britain Together: a national strategy for neighbourhood renewal*, HMSO, 1998, p9

# Nine
# Equalities and poverty
*Rona Fitzgerald, European Policies Research Centre*

## Introduction

Social inclusion is one of the founding objectives of the Scottish Executive and the Scottish Parliament. In November 1999, the Scottish Executive published the social justice report, *Social Justice: a Scotland where everyone matters*, setting out ten long-term targets for the achievement of social justice, and 29 milestones marking progress towards the targets. In addition, it made a commitment to publishing an annual Scottish social justice report to begin the process of what it termed *measuring what matters* in terms of social justice. Alongside this commitment to social inclusion, the Executive has outlined its plan for achieving equality through mainstreaming equality in public policy. Following extensive consultation, the *Equality Strategy* was published in November 2000.[1] The move to mainstreaming signals a shift in the mechanism for achieving equality. This commitment to bring an equality perspective to bear on mainstream policy making and implementation provided a changed context for the pursuit of equality in Scotland.

However, there is a lack of clarity about the relationship between the pursuit of social justice and equality; both are considered important strands of the Executive's strategic intervention. What is not clear is whether the *Equality Strategy* represents an *overarching* framework for the achievement of equality and social justice in Scotland and how these strategic objectives intersect and complement one another. One of the common challenges of the complex sectoral system of departmental policy making and implementation that operates in Scotland, is the question of *joined-up government*. This challenge is acute in an evolving area of practice such as mainstreaming, but it is crucial that the issue of policy coherence is addressed at the early stage.

## Delivering the strategy

The social inclusion strategy is being delivered through partnerships comprised of local authorities, economic development agencies, the private sector, and voluntary and community representatives. In addition, a range of other policy interventions are delivered at national and local level, and through European Union funds aimed at tackling regional disparities and promoting growth and social integration and participation. Feedback from work undertaken on the social inclusion partnerships in Glasgow suggests that current functioning represents a new way of working. The change to partnership needs to be supported; many of the partners/ agencies already have their own working methods and are not used to more participative practices nor are they used to being accountable. Because the partnerships are at different stages and have different experiences and histories, they have concentrated on different things. Nevertheless, there is a common pattern of work in the last few years. The main focus has been on developing partnership working and putting structures in place – trying to relate targets and outputs, providing baseline data, developing a strategic approach to funding, and promoting community ownership of the strategies.[2] In the context of the social inclusion partnerships, the issue of support and resources for mainstreaming is crucial. There is considerable competition for resources in the area-based strategies; there is also a challenge in terms of how the partner organisations view mainstreaming as an approach and adopt it for all of their policy interventions.

## Mainstreaming

Strategies for equality and inclusion have been refined over the last thirty years as greater priority has been given to the achievement of economic and social cohesion. In the UK, the commitment to equal opportunities has most often been translated into practice through positive action measures to enable women to overcome the barriers that many face in accessing services, training and the labour market. In the 1990s the mainstreaming approach was elaborated in a number of fora including the UN and the European Union. Mainstreaming is a strategy that aims to make equality considerations a regular part of the mainstream policy process. It entails building in equality rather than building it onto existing policies and programmes. Much of the evolving practice in this area relates to main-streaming gender equality, as a convincing case has been put forward for using gender as a lens that can also reflect other factors such as race and disability.[3] Underlying the concept of mainstreaming gender equality is a recognition that women and men do not have the same situations, needs and resources. A further implicit acknowledgement is that while real gains have been made in terms of legislation outlawing gender discrimination, the achievement of equality requires a shift or transformation in the policy making process, recognising how gender as a factor structures opportunities from labour market participation to access to services. In the Scottish policy context, mainstreaming entails the application of an equality filter/lens to all aspects of policy making from strategy development and policy formulation through to monitoring and evaluation. Mainstreaming also offers an important link with the sustainability of economic and social cohesion by adopting a social justice approach to potentially economic and socially divisive inequalities.

## Poverty and equality

In the UK, the impetus to tackle social exclusion is based on a notion of geographical/area-based or group disadvantage. For example, it targets areas with high incidence of poverty or specific groups like the young unemployed. While the notion of social inclusion communicates an imperative around equal opportunities, the analysis underpinning this concept ignores the different experience of men and women in respect of poverty and social exclusion. Women are more likely to be living in poverty than men both at UK level and in Scotland. In addition, the extent of the poverty and deprivation can be hidden in data that is collected without using gender as a frame of reference or analysis.[4] The Scottish Household Survey[5] was commisioned to provide detailed data to underpin the social inclusion strategy. The 2001 survey provided a number of useful key points in relation to the relative position of women and men:

- Households with a female highest income householder (HIH) are less likely than those with a male HIH to have a bank account, savings and investments, or home contents insurance.

- Households with a male HIH are more likely to be buying their homes with a mortgage or loan, while households with a female HIH are more likely to be renting from a social landlord.
- Households with a female HIH are more likely than those with a male HIH to be dependent on state benefits.
- Sixty-two per cent of women of working age are in employment (self-employed or working full or part time), compared with 71 per cent of men of working age.
- Married women are more likely to be in part-time employment than women in any other marital status group.

The manner in which data is collected on women and poverty is hampered by the following structural inadequacies: an absence of gender disaggregation and analysis of the information; the use of the 'household' rather than the individual as the primary unit of analysis – there is a case for the collection of data on both levels; an absence of data on the manner in which income is distributed within the household; and the problem of providing a comprehensive gender analysis of the data when the deprivation index utilised is not constructed with a view to facilitating a gender analysis.

Fundamental to this issue is the use of the household as the basic unit for analysis. This assumes that all resources of the household are shared equally and that all individuals within the household have equal access to those resources. Research in Ireland underlined the way in which data collection and analysis can hide the extent of poverty and deprivation for women.[6]

## Subsidiarity?

Issues around what might be called *subsidiarity* – the best level for matters to be dealt with – are crucial to acknowledge and resolve. For example, one of the key requirements to underpin a mainstreaming strategy is reliable and comprehensive data. The most rational way to collect that is through the statistical authorities at Scottish and UK level. Effective mainstreaming necessitates both *embedded understanding* and *capacity for application* within the responsible departments and agencies and within the communities of interest. The need for capacity building is clear but it needs to be tailored to sectoral, community and institutional needs. It is necessary for all those involved to take a proactive approach to building capacity in this area.

## Issues for consideration

Conceptual clarity is essential for the achievement of equality and for the credibility of a mainstreaming strategy. The notion of mainstreaming is based on the acceptance of diversity – recognising the different needs, resources and situations of the communities of interest in the Scottish policy community. It can be a progressive strategy with a capacity to contribute to greater equality. However, there needs to be mobilisation around what is 'progress', how and why it represents progress and how this progress is to be measured. In respect of the social inclusion imperative and the equalities agenda, the key challenge is to establish conceptual clarity and to identify how resources can be shared and maximised in developing the capacity to mainstream equality in the Scottish policy processes.

### Notes

1   *Equality Strategy: working together for equality*, Scottish Executive, 2000
2   R Fitzgerald, *Engendering the Work of the SIPs in Glasgow: gender impact assessment and its application to social inclusion*, Report for Glasgow Women and Social Inclusion Working Group, 2001
3   EGGE, EC Expert Group on Gender and Employment, 2001
4   See note 2
5   *Scottish Household Survey*, Bulletin No 5, Scottish Executive, 2001
6   *Out of Sight: the hidden poverty of women*, NWCI Policy Discussion Paper, 2001

# Ten

# Poverty and asylum seekers

*Iain Ferguson, Department of Applied Social Science, University of Sterling*

## Legal context: the Immigration and Asylum Act 1999

Since 1999, asylum seekers in Britain have experienced a form of welfare apartheid. As a result of the Immigration and Asylum Act introduced in that year, they are excluded from the mainstream social security system, while in Scotland the duty to promote social welfare, imposed on local authority social work departments by the 1968 Social Work (Scotland) Act, does not apply to those seeking asylum. (As asylum and immigration are areas reserved for the Westminster Parliament under the devolution settlement, the Immigration and Asylum Act also applies to Scotland.) Policy in this area has sometimes been described as a 'Dutch auction', in which the two main political parties seek to outdo each other in the harshness of their treatment of those fleeing war, persecution or extreme poverty. In this respect, the 1999 Act – New Labour's response to the 'problem' of asylum seekers – trumps not only previous Conservative legislation but is also much harsher than the policies of most other European states.[1] The policy underpinning the Act has three main aspects:[2]

- **Increased deportation and detention**
  As well as the opening of several new detention centres since 1997 (including the first in Scotland, at the former Dungavel prison), the number of people being deported has increased under New Labour, from three an hour in 1997 to five an hour in 2001.

- **The introduction of vouchers**
  Under previous Conservative governments, local authorities had responsibility for providing assistance to families seeking asylum but

could only do so 'in kind' to single asylum seekers without children. New Labour has extended this cashless support to all asylum seekers, through the introduction of a voucher system. Vouchers are set at 70 per cent of income support rate, with 10 per cent redeemable in cash. The scheme is administered by Sodexho, a multinational company, which has promoted the scheme to retailers and supermarkets as 'a revenue-raising opportunity', since asylum seekers are not entitled to change from these vouchers (see p122).

- **Dispersal**
  Under a scheme administered by the National Asylum Support Service (NASS), asylum seekers are now compulsorily dispersed to different areas of the country, regardless of whether or not they have family and friends there. Under the policy of dispersal, Scotland is expected to receive up to 15,000 asylum seekers by the end of 2004, with the over-whelming majority of these coming to Glasgow. In a contract entered into with NASS in April 2000, Glasgow City Council has undertaken to provide 2,000 units of family accommodation and 500 units of accommodation for single people from its housing stock. By the summer of 2001, around 4,500 people had taken up residence in Glasgow. On average, the city is accommodating 20 new families a week and 10 new single people a week.[3]

Despite initial claims by the Home Office that asylum seekers would be sent to 'cluster zones' that were 'multi-ethnic', in practice price and the availability of cheap housing appear to have been the main driving forces. In Glasgow, the majority have been housed in Sighthill, an area of extreme deprivation in the north of the city. The failure to explain to existing residents in Sighthill the circumstances from which the asylum seekers were fleeing, or to provide additional resources to a desperately poor area which would lead to the newly-arrived asylum seekers being seen as a welcome addition rather than a threat, and against the background of a hostile tabloid press, led to a significant increase in racist attacks during the summer of 2001 and to the murder of a young Turkish Kurd, Firsat Dag.

## Administration of policy

Under the 1999 legislation, responsibility for asylum seekers has been removed from the control of democratically-elected local councils and been placed with NASS. NASS operates through local consortia and in Scotland the consortium is run by an executive made up of nominees from housing, social work, education, health and the police along with representatives from the Scottish Federation of Housing Associations and the Scottish Refugee Council.

## Effectiveness of current policy

In considering the 'effectiveness' of current asylum seeker policy in relation to poverty, it is important to understand the assumptions underpinning that policy, and its rationale. The central assumption, for which there is no evidence but which is repeatedly voiced by both main political parties and much of the media, is that it is cash benefits which attract asylum seekers to Britain, and that Britain is perceived as 'a soft touch' by 'economic migrants' seeking to improve their standard of living. By contrast:

> 'Experience has shown that [provision in kind] is less attractive and provides less of a financial inducement for those who would be drawn by a cash scheme.'[4]

The Act therefore has a deterrent intention, through making life as an asylum seeker in Britain as unattractive as possible. In this sense, as Cohen[5] has noted, the Act can be seen as a return to the Poor Law, both in its punitive ethos and also in that it removes asylum seekers entirely from the rights and protections they would be entitled to within the social security system, however limited they might be.[6]

## The impact on health

Both the voucher and dispersal systems have been shown to be profoundly detrimental to the health and well-being of asylum seekers and their children. The British Medical Association, in conjunction with the Medical Foundation for the Care of Victims of Torture, has produced a dossier of evidence outlining cases where doctors believe that government policy has affected the well-being of asylum seekers. The two main conclusions of the study were first, that the voucher system should be scrapped in favour of cash benefits in line with income support, and second, that the dispersal policy should be overhauled, with the aim of protecting asylum seekers and not punishing them.[7] A study of the mental health needs of asylum seekers in Glasgow came to similar conclusions.[8] In this study, the voucher system was identified by asylum seeker respondents as the biggest problem they faced. A whole range of problems were associated with vouchers: the level at which they are set, which leaves most asylum seekers in extreme poverty; the fact that they are not entitled to change from the vouchers, forcing them to go round supermarkets with a calculator; the fact that they can only be used at a limited number of outlets, preventing asylum seekers from taking advantage of sales or using cheaper outlets; and finally, the humiliation involved in their use, likened by some to the Yellow Star imposed on Jews by the Nazis. Through an interpreter, an Iranian woman in Sighthill expressed her feelings about vouchers:

'The worst thing she has experienced is the vouchers, and she is saying it is a nightmare. It is terrible, it is the worst thing that you could ever imagine… She is saying that she doesn't go to shops as she wishes to, because she remembers she has to present a voucher and everybody will look at her differently. When, for instance, she spends £3, she doesn't get the change and obviously she loses here, and because there is hardly any money, she cannot afford to lose £2. So she is saying that once a week, she goes to shop and does all her shopping at once, because she just hates to present the voucher.'[9]

Nor do most asylum seekers have any choice about receiving vouchers. Despite the fact that many are highly qualified, and would want to work, they are not permitted to work until they have been in this country for six months, while dependants of asylum seekers are forbidden to take up employment until such time as the asylum seeker receives a positive decision on his or her claim for asylum.

## Issues for anti-poverty work

A number of factors make anti-poverty work with this group of people particularly challenging. First, in terms of benefits advice, the 1999 Act seeks to establish a closed system of welfare provision outside the social security system and incapable of legal challenge, where the only possible means of support for asylum seekers are contained within the Act itself.[10] Second, the close inter-relationship between welfare entitlement and immigration legislation means that welfare advisers need to work in close co-operation with immigration advisers. Third, the newness of the Act (and the fact that the legislation is likely to be significantly amended during 2002) means that there is still a good deal of uncertainty about the possibilities for challenge. In terms of wider anti-poverty work, however, there is considerable scope for the use of a community development approach to address the wide range of health and social problems faced by asylum seekers in Glasgow.[11] Given that many of these problems are also shared by existing local residents in the areas to which asylum seekers have been dispersed, there is scope for a united response involving local people and asylum seekers to address community problems, a response which can also help remove the basis for racism in these areas.

## Update

Policy in relation to asylum seekers is changing very rapidly at both British and European level and a number of major policy changes are imminent. In terms of Britain, a new White Paper *Secure Borders, Safe Haven* was introduced by Home Secretary David Blunkett in February 2002, and has laid the basis for the Immigration, Asylum and Nationality Bill currently going through the Westminster Parliament. This is the fourth major revision of asylum legislation in ten years. In respect of poverty issues, following a campaign involving a wide range of organisations and prominent individuals, the hated voucher system is to be removed and replaced by a system of cash benefits. While this change is to be welcomed since it removes the stigma which vouchers involved, it does not affect the material situation of asylum seekers, since cash benefits will continue to be paid at 70 per cent of income support levels. The provisions of the Bill include the greater use of compulsory accommodation, the reduction of the right to appeal against refusal of asylum claims and the provision of segregated education for the children of asylum seekers. These measures can be seen as a response by New Labour to the electoral successes of far right parties in Britain and Europe and an attempt to undermine them by stealing their policies. Others (including the representatives of the Swedish Government at the Seville Conference on Immigration and Asylum in June 2002) have argued, however, that adopting the policies of the far right only serves to increase their credibility, as well as leading to a neglect of the rights of those seeking asylum. As the Refugee Council has noted in its response to the White Paper:

> 'The asylum aspects…concentrate on the control and removal of rejected asylum seekers. The real purpose of the system, to provide protection to refugees, is largely neglected.'[12]

## Notes

1 M Lavalette, G Mooney, E Mynott, K Evans and B Richardson, 'The Woeful Record of the House of Blair', *International Socialism*, 90, 2001, pp77-102

2 S Cohen, *Immigration Controls, the Family and the Welfare State*, Jessica Kingsley Publishers, 2001

3 SASC, *Asylum Briefing*, Summer 2001

4 See note 2

5 See note 2

6 E Mynott, 'Analysing the Creation of Apartheid for Asylum Seekers in the UK', *Community, Work and Family*, 3(3), 2000, pp311-331

7 BMA/Medical Foundation for the Treatment of Victims of Torture, *Asylum Seekers and Health*, BMA, 2001

8 I Ferguson and A Barclay, *Seeking Peace of Mind: the mental health needs of asylum seekers in Glasgow*, University of Stirling, 2002

9 See note 8

10 See note 2

11 A Rosengard, I Laing and A Jackson, *The Housing and Related Support Needs of Asylum Seekers and Refugees in Scotland: implications of the Immigration and Asylum Act 1999*, Background and Briefing Paper for the Scottish Refugee Council, 2000

12 *Response to the White Paper, 'Secure Borders, Safe Haven'*, Refugee Council, 2002

# Eleven
## Poverty and welfare
*Morag Gillespie, Citizens Rights and Advice, Fife*

### Introduction

In the welfare rights field, there were expectations of significant change with the election of the Labour Government in 1997. The Prime Minister's stated policy objective of eradicating child poverty over twenty years raised hopes of at least some progressive changes in the welfare and social security field. Although most social security policy and spending decisions remain with the Westminster government, the debate around free personal care for the elderly has highlighted the scope for the Scottish Parliament to change the approach and priorities for policy in Scotland.

There have been many changes in social security policy in the last four to five years, which those seeking to claim benefits and their advisers alike have been hard-pressed to keep up with. However, the key question is whether welfare and social security changes are making a difference – are they having an impact in reducing poverty and disadvantage?

### Making work pay

A key part of the Government's approach is to make work pay. The introduction of a modest minimum wage and taxation and national insurance reform would have had a limited effect on their own, but the new working families' tax credit (WFTC), which replaced family credit, takes account of certain childcare costs in the childcare tax credit (confusingly not a separate benefit, but part of WFTC) and has allowed more people in poorly paid work to use childcare. Anecdotal evidence from advice workers is that the greatest positive change for lone parents from this new benefit has been the decision to disregard maintenance payments. A significant number of the problems advice workers come up against are less with the benefit itself, but more as a consequence of payment through the wage packet. These include enforced reductions in hours and dismissals, often in small businesses. Some, albeit a minority, may have ended up worse off as a result.

The less generous treatment of childcare costs in housing and council tax benefits, combined with the loss of other concessions and entitlements such as free school meals, has devalued the gains from WFTC for many low wage earners who face a high marginal rate of taxation as these benefits and entitlements have been reduced or stopped. Another paradox of the new scheme is that, because of the relative generosity of WFTC, more people are entitled to the benefit, but are then drawn into high marginal rates of taxation.

Although it is too early to be sure of its effects, there is some early evidence that, overall, lone parents in particular are benefiting from these changes.[1] However, compulsory interviews about work from 2002 will increase the pressure on lone parents to work regardless of their own judgement of whether it is appropriate for them.

Before we know it, the current tax credits system will be history – a new scheme from April 2003 will include awards for a full tax year that are based on evidence for the whole of the previous tax year.[2] The details are not yet clear, but advice workers will need to brace themselves for a new set of challenges in seeking to provide advice, support and advocacy for people of working age.

## Disability benefits

There is little evidence of the disabled person's tax credit being of significantly greater benefit to people with disabilities than its predecessor, disability working allowance – the qualifying conditions are still very difficult to meet and, to state the obvious, there remains the uphill task of gaining employment in the first place.

For many people with disabilities, work remains an unrealistic option and claiming benefits such as disability living allowance (DLA) and, to a lesser extent, attendance allowance, remains an enduring challenge for them and their representatives. Although the Government may be seeking to improve the quality of decision making in DLA claims, the need to take claims to appeal seems to have become a matter of routine. The fact that a high success rate is achieved on appeal, particularly where representation is provided,[3] suggests that there remain fundamental problems with these benefits. A more effective and fair way of addressing the extra costs of disability and the needs of people with disabilities remains an area for urgent future development.

## Pensions and other benefits on retirement

The Government has been slow to make inroads in addressing another key policy aim – that of ending pensioner poverty. Modest changes in the first four years have been replaced by more significant increases in the basic state retirement pension in 2001 and 2002. The introduction of a minimum income guarantee (MIG) for pensioners that is linked to earnings, along with increased savings limits, should help to reduce the numbers of pensioners living in poverty. Whether a new scheme with a new name will reduce the stigma attached to means-tested benefits remains to be seen. However, what seems more certain is that the MIG and the new pension credit scheme planned for 2003 will increase reliance on means-tested benefits while the basic state pension continues to be tied to the retail price index. The National Pensioners Confederation has said that the MIG:

> 'Coupled with the pension credit proposals to take into account the amount of individual savings will result in 5.5 million pensioners (half the pensioner population) facing some form of means-testing by 2003.'[4]

## Housing costs

Many of the improvements identified above can be reduced in value because of their interaction with housing benefit (HB) and council tax benefit (CTB). The high rate of withdrawal as income increases remains a source of disappointment for many as they see gains in one area pared away through lost benefits for housing costs. However, another priority policy area, that of reducing benefit fraud, is causing significant stress and distress for those claiming and their advisers alike.

Local authorities administer HB and CTB claims. For a host of reasons, including the recent requirement to put in place a new verification framework that aims to reduce overpayments and fraud, the ability of councils across Scotland to process claims appropriately and within target time scales has proved seriously lacking.[5] In Fife, advice agencies in Fife Rights Forum decided to monitor what was identified as a growing problem. Evidence to date shows that in some cases, council officials, tenants and their advisers are arguing over whether the appropriate claims and forms have been completed and handed in, while another department is recording mounting rent arrears and, in extreme cases, beginning proceedings for eviction. All of this is happening while the decision about a claim is awaited. Although the number of people affected may not be large, the impact is enormous on everyone caught up in the process. This example highlights that anti-fraud measures must not be the main drivers in benefits administration; rather the first priority should be to ensure entitlements are paid. This is a balance that the Government is not yet getting right.

## Asylum seekers

For asylum seekers in Scotland and elsewhere in the UK, there are several issues around benefits entitlements that continue to add to the stresses they face. The notorious vouchers system for benefits payments was replaced in April 2002 by a cash-based system. Asylum seekers will continue to receive vouchers but these will be exchangeable for cash rather than goods.[6] However, CPAG has pointed out that although the change is welcome, payments are still much lower than income support – an asylum seeker over the age of 29 receives only £37.77 a week.[7] As yet, the Government has given no formal commitment to annual uprating of voucher values.

Even when asylum seekers manage finally to gain a positive decision and, in theory, have the same right to access benefits, they continue to face long delays in accessing benefits. The National Asylum Support Service (NASS) can continue to support for a period of 28 days (14 days until April 2002), but few receive payments within that period – the (then) Benefits Agency reported that more than 50 per cent are taking more than six weeks. Even with the extended support from NASS, there is a clear need for the (then) Benefits Agency to improve the quality and speed of decision making in such cases and, where there are delays, provide for interim payments to be made.

## Looking forward

There are a number of areas of progress in social security policy, particularly in addressing in-work poverty, even if the scale of the impact may be less than hoped for.[8] Some issues, such as free personal care for the elderly and benefit fraud, have been hotly debated in Scotland. However, the increased reliance on means-testing combines with the failure to address the high end of income inequalities to give cause for some concern about the capacity to make progress in reducing inequalities and reducing poverty, particularly for those not in paid work. Modest benefit uprating of 1.7 per cent from October 2002 will only reinforce the gap compared with earnings. Meantime, the repayment of debts and social fund loans mean that many on income support, predominantly lone parents and people with disabilities,[9] may be living on much less than people imagine. The report card on tackling poverty should probably read – good start but there is plenty of room for improvement.

### Notes

1   M Brewer and P Gregg, 'Lone Parents, the Working Families' Tax Credit and Employment in Households with Children', in R Dickens, J Wadsworth and P Gregg (eds), *The State of Working Britain, Update*, Centre for Economic Performance, 2001

2   P Treloar, 'The Tax Credits Bill', *Welfare Rights Bulletin*, February 2002, No 166, pp4-5

3   M McKeown, 'Welfare Rights and Regeneration', *SCOLAG*, October 2001, pp177-179

4   NPC Briefing No 23, November 2001

5   For example, 'Council's Blunders Threaten Eviction for Tenants', *SCOLAG*, July 2001, No 285, p118

6   'Asylum Support Update', *LASA Review*, No 92, LASA, April 2002

7   'Something Cheery for Asylum Seekers', *Campaigns Newsletter*, No 21, Child Poverty Action Group, April 2002

8   For example, P Townsend, 'Anti-poverty Policy: A bit rich?', *The Guardian*, 9 March 2001

9   *Income Support Quarterly Statistical Enquiry*, November 2001, Table 12.3, p116

# Twelve
## Poverty and low pay
*John Wilson, Scottish Low Pay Unit*

Low pay has long been recognised as a major cause of poverty. The Labour Government introduced the national minimum wage in its first term. For the first time, workers in Britain aged 18 and over were entitled to a legal minimum wage regardless of what part of the country they lived in or the size of the organisation they worked for. It was a significant step in the battle against low pay and poverty. However:

> 'There is a long way to go before the problem of in-work poverty is solved and the progress towards a real living wage and towards economic equality between men and women remains painfully slow.'[1]

## The national minimum wage

The national minimum wage has increased each year since it was introduced; the starting figure was set at a 'compromise' level that was arrived at to ensure there was no backlash from employers. The minimum wage rates introduced were well below those advocated by the trade unions and the Scottish Low Pay Unit (or indeed the European Parliament). The current (July 2002) rate stands at £3.50 for 18–21-year- olds and £4.10 for those over 22 years. In setting these new rates in October 2001 the Government also proposed that further increases should be introduced in October 2002. The proposed figures give an increase of 2.4 per cent, equivalent to only 10 pence an hour. Even this meagre increase is tempered with the statement that it 'will be dependent on the economic circumstances of the time'.

These national minimum wage rates and the increases should be considered in comparison to other groups. Someone on the national minimum wage, based on working a 40-hour week, will earn approximately £8,000 per annum. The proposed increase in October 2002 will deliver an annual increase of £200. If we take the current average wage in Scotland being at a level of £23,500 and current pay settlements averaging at 3 per cent, this represents an annual increase of £705. MSP's pay award in early 2002 of 13.5 per cent means that they will receive an annual increase of £6,000.

These differences in pay illustrate one of the fundamental issues relating to low pay and earnings. That is, if pay structures continue to be settled on percentage awards then those on the lowest earnings will see their incomes decrease year-on-year compared with those on higher income levels.

> 'Uprating the minimum wage above the level of £4.10 would be a first step towards achieving a decent minimum wage. In the longer term the Government must make an automatic link between average earnings and increases in the minimum wage.'[2]

The national minimum wage established two levels: for those 18–21-year-olds (sometimes called the development rate) and for workers over 22 (called the standard rate). Within these age groups there is also a lower minimum wage level for those participating in recognised training schemes. However, the Government failed to tackle the issue of the minimum wage for those aged 16 and 17 years. The Scottish Low Pay Unit, along with the trade unions, has consistently argued against a separate minimum wage for young workers. There has never been any justification for paying workers doing the same job different rates simply on the grounds of age.

## Working families' tax credit

In anticipation of the problems faced by workers on low incomes, the Government revamped the in-work benefit, family credit, and introduced the working families' tax credit (WFTC), which through sleight of hand shifted the responsibility for in-work benefits from the Benefits Agency to the Inland Revenue. (This change took place mainly to tackle other economic criteria that the Government was attempting to meet in relation to its European monetary policies.)

By its very nature, the continued dependence on WFTC to supplement income levels of workers clearly shows that the present levels of pay packet rewards for work are not enough to sustain workers and their families and that the Government must provide financial support to supplement earnings levels – thereby in the process subsidising low-paying employers. This practice will prove increasingly expensive for the Government.

## Creating low-paid work

Despite ongoing attempts by government both at UK and at Scottish Executive level to introduce new employment opportunities through inward investment, many of the jobs created continue to be either at the low end of the pay scale or part-time employment in the services sector, a problem that continues to be acute in some of the older industrial centres, such as Glasgow. Even in the much heralded 'new technology' and call centre industries, the earning levels are not nearly enough to avoid the necessity of sole family earners claiming WFTC to provide what approaches a reasonable income level to meet family costs.

Even within the industries promoted as providing future economic strength for Scotland (such as electronics and the so-called 'knowledge' sectors) there has been uncertainty about future employment prospects and redundancies. The examples of Motorola closing down its Bathgate manufacturing base, and the announcement in 2002 by BT that it intends to reduce the number of call centre jobs, suggest that in at least two key areas of the Scottish economy the future does not look at all bright. In other parts of the economy, manufacturing has continued to decline with further redundancies in shipbuilding, engineering and defence related work.

## Tackling in-work poverty: prospects and policies

The role of the Scottish Executive and Parliament is limited in addressing employment matters, especially income measures such as the national minimum wage and WFTC, since these are reserved issues to Westminster. However, the Scottish Executive does play a key role through inward investment and business growth strategies; these areas could yield the potential to place an onus on employers setting up business in Scotland to introduce employment terms and conditions that are more 'worker-friendly' than those currently set through the national minimum wage.

While the Government should be applauded for introducing the national minimum wage and reviewing the WFTC, it has still got a long way to go to prove it is serious about tackling the increasing differentials between those on low-wage incomes and those earning above average earnings and beyond. Much more needs to be done to address the on-going problems of the rich getting richer and poor becoming more dis-advantaged – the problem of increasing social polarisation – a theme that is reflected in a number of the other essays in this collection.

Although, as yet, no attempt has been made here to tackle the question of benefits to those who are unemployed, or unable to find suit-able employment, we should be concerned about the increasing spate of references made by government ministers to 'workless families', indicat-ing that the only solution to people on benefits to increase their incomes is through finding 'work', defined as paid employment. Such attitudes ignore those who do unpaid work and the fact that paid employment is insecure, transient and often unavailable.

People taking up employment find they are entering an increasingly volatile and uncertain labour market, with an increase in the so-called 'contract culture', short-term contracts, part-time and sessional work often being the only employment available. In July 2000, the UK govern-ment implemented improved rights for part-time workers, which gave them many of the same employment rights as full-time employees. While much more remains to be done to address the problems being faced by this group of workers, such policy developments represent welcome advances for groups of vulnerable workers, especially low-paid female workers.

In conclusion, there have been major advances in relation to the question of low pay and these should not be ignored or underestimated. However, the problem of low wages and of the 'working poor' remains one of the major features of poverty throughout Britain and Scotland today. The introduction of the national minimum wage is a step on the right road but much remains to be done, in particular scrapping the youth development rate, linking future increases to movements in average earn-ings, improving enforcement of the minimum wage, and setting up an independent uprating mechanism.

### Notes

1   P Kelly and R Harris, *Towards a Living Wage*, Scottish Low Pay Unit, 2001
2   See note 1

# Thirteen
# The New Deal
*Leaza McSorley, Glasgow Caledonian University*

The New Deal is the cornerstone of New Labour's 'welfare to work' pro-gramme. It is an active employment policy which was initially only for unemployed people aged 18 to 24, but has been extended to cover the long-term unemployed aged over 25, lone parents and disabled people.

The programme has been deemed successful. The Government's (1997) manifesto target to get 250,000 young unemployed people off benefits and into work had been exceeded by September 2000 and approximately 352,000 had found employment by March 2002. Of these around 280,000 were classified as 'sustained' jobs.[1] Since the New Deal for young people began, 85,500 have started the programme in Scotland: 40,700 have gone into jobs and 30,700 of these were sustained jobs.[2] The destinations of those leaving the New Deal in Scotland are as follows: 40 per cent went into unsubsidised employment, 14 per cent went onto other benefits, 22 per cent went to other known destinations and the des-tination of 24 per cent is unknown.

The success of the programme has undoubtedly been aided by the strong economy and tight labour market conditions: many of those on the New Deal would have found work without the New Deal, although it may have taken them longer.

However, there have been concerns expressed regarding the sus-tainability of some of the jobs obtained by New Deal participants.[3] Recent research from The Work Foundation has found that:

> 'Over the period for which core performance data is available, roughly half of those leaving the New Deal for a job went back onto jobseeker's allowance within six months.'[4]

Evidence from Glasgow suggests that in 2000/01 around 15,000 people took part in all the various employment programmes in Glasgow:

'As many as 9,000-10,000 of them were back on the dole again not long afterwards, with nothing to do but wait their turn to go round again.'[5]

This may appear to contradict the Government's claim that three-quarters of young people leaving the New Deal for work have found 'sustained' employment. However, sustained employment is defined as a job that lasts more than 13 weeks there is also an employer subsidy of £60 per week for six months. It is therefore unsurprising that three-quarters of New Deal jobs last longer than 13 weeks.

The destination of 24 per cent of all clients leaving the New Deal in Scotland is unknown and of the 3,670 young people starting on the sub-sidised employment option the destination of 72 per cent of them is unknown.[6] These figures appear to confirm the Work Foundation's fear 'that we have a group of people spinning around in the New Deal like a ball of fluff in a washing machine'.[7]

## Closed door or revolving door?

The 'low pay – no pay cycle'[8] has long been recognised as characteristic of the low-wage labour market. The fact that many of the New Deal par-ticipants are alternating between low pay, unemployment and New Deal participation 'would perhaps be less of a cause for concern if the low-paid jobs are a stepping stone to higher paid jobs. But they do not appear to be.'[9] This view is confirmed by Stewart:

'Low-paid jobs are more likely to act as blind alleys than as stepping stones to positions higher up the pay distribution.'[10]

The low pay – no pay cycle is of course 'symptomatic not of a failure of the New Deal but of the nature of the low-tech end of the service sec-tor employment itself'.[11] The nature of many of the jobs created in this new economy remain at the bottom end of the skills and wage scale and while long periods of unemployment when young do harm future earn-ings potential, there is little evidence that regularly 'churning' between low-wage, low-skill jobs and unemployment is any more beneficial.

## The New Deal – phase two

Concern has also been raised about the effectiveness of the New Deal in the most deprived areas and in helping the least 'job-ready' into work. The Government recognised these deficiencies in its Green Paper, *Towards Full Employment in a Modern Society*, published in 2001. The paper sets out the key priorities for the second phase of the New Deal: an 'employer-led' programme to match better the needs of employers with the training of the New Deal participants; extra provision for the 'least job-ready' and a focus on the most deprived areas that have benefited least from the New Deal in the past.

Greater employer involvement is viewed as the key to achieving the aims of the second phase and the programme is to become: 'demand-led. This means placing employers at the centre of the New Deal system – as designers, key customers and end users.' However, employers' willingness to take on the most disadvantaged participants (for example, those with literacy/drug-addiction problems) has not been apparent and the trend is that employers are increasingly demanding job-ready candidates.[12]

The second part of the strategy for getting the most disadvantaged into jobs is the increasing role of mandatory participation and the use of sanctions. Benefit sanctions can be imposed, for example, for not attending a meeting with a personal adviser: 19,344 people in Britain suffered benefit sanctions in 2000/01. The use of New Deal sanctions is highest in the most depressed regions with the highest job deficits. A report from the then Department for Education and Employment concluded that 'sanctions impose real hardship' and identified the groups most likely to suffer benefit loss as: people from minority ethnic communities; those with caring responsibilities; and people with health problems.[13]

The new mandatory structure of the New Deal is epitomised in the StepUp pilot programme, to be run in six areas of Britain (including East Ayrshire). In this programme those who do not enter employment within six months of leaving the New Deal will be allocated jobs with a local employer. They will receive pay at the minimum wage level and the programme will be subsidised by the Government. If a job is refused, benefits will be stopped. StepUp is supported with mandatory work preparation classes and non-attendance will also result in benefit loss.[14] The Chancellor highlighted StepUp in his budget speech as a programme that 'will oblige the long-term unemployed to accept a guaranteed job'.

The aim of the second phase of the New Deal is to 'broaden the scope of welfare to work programmes to cover all people on benefits who are economically inactive'.[15] The Government's target of increasing the number of lone parents in work by 20 per cent to 70 per cent within the next ten years may also indicate the greater use of compulsion for all who claim benefits and are of working age, though at present lone parents must only attend initial interviews. The New Deal for those over 25 years old will also become compulsory, 'with benefit sanctions of up to six months for those who refuse to take part'.[16]

However the causes of unemployment and labour market inactivity are somewhat more complex than 'workshy layabouts' who can be forced into work. For example, in areas where the New Deal has been least successful there are between six and twelve unemployed people wanting a job for every vacancy. Simply, there are not enough jobs and none of the proposals put forward in the Government's Green Paper will overcome this problem. Also, 16 per cent of New Deal participants in Scotland have literacy and numeracy problems;[17] stopping benefits will not rectify this. It appears that the Government intends to be tough on unemployment but, not, unfortunately, on the causes of unemployment.

## Policy solutions

The welfare to work policies have so far only focused on the supply-side problems in the labour market. But supply-side policies alone will achieve little except punishing the most deprived people in the country because they happen to live in a deprived area. There is a need for fully developed demand-side policies to aid job creation and retention in the most deprived areas and the time to produce results before any mandatory aspects of the New Deal are introduced.

The role of employers in the New Deal must also be re-examined. For example, the New Deal Task force wish to see employers as 'designers, key customers and end users' of the New Deal, but why not as training providers? Presently employers receive a weekly subsidy of £60 for taking on a New Deal participant but are under no obligation to provide training. An additional sum of £750 is available, over six months, to employers who provide accredited training. This must be built upon with employers only receiving a subsidy if they provide accredited training, preferably for at least a one-year period. This will not only increase the employability of the worker but will benefit the employer through increased productivity and staff retention. Employers' expectations that the New Deal will provide them with job-ready candidates must be altered by convincing them of the benefits of providing in-work training themselves.

## Conclusion

It is clear that unemployment benefits are no longer a universal right but instead are to be used to control the behaviour of the working-age population of this country. Plans for the second phase of the New Deal seem to indicate that in the future, the New Deal will no longer be an active employment policy but a compulsory employment policy.

Denying people the right to a basic subsistence income because of their non-compliant behaviour will not only be ineffective at getting people back to work; it is immoral. It also sets the precedence for future developments of the welfare state, for example, a Scotland where smokers are denied medical treatment because they refused to participate in a healthy lifestyle regime now does not seem so inconceivable.

### Notes

1   www.employmentservice.gov.uk
2   Scottish Executive, 2002
3   Westwood *et al*, *Full Employment and the New Deal*, The Work Foundation, 2002
4   S Martin, 'Free the PA!' in Westwood *et al*, *Full Employment and the New Deal*, The Work Foundation, 2002
5   B Marshall, 'Glasgow: a full employment city?' in Westwood *et al*, *Full Employment and the New Deal*, The Work Foundation, 2002
6   See note 2
7   A Sinclair and A Westwood, 'Policy versus Process', in Westwood *et al*, *Full Employment and the New Deal*, The Work Foundation, 2002
8   D Metcalf, *The Way Out? Low pay and the services sector*, CentrePiece,1999
9   See note 8
10  M Stewart, 'Low Pay in Britain: piecing together the picture', in P Gregg and J Wadsworth (eds), *The State of Working Britain*, Manchester University Press, 1999
11  J Philpott, 'An Employer-led New Deal?' in Westwood *et al*, *Full Employment and the New Deal*, The Work Foundation, 2002

12 See note 3

13 J Williamson, 'Work for a Pittance or Else', *The Guardian*, 26 April 2002

14 See note 13

15 Department for Education and Employment, *Towards Full Employment in a Modern Society*, The Stationery Office, 2001

16 See note 15

17 See note 2

# Fourteen
# From the public to the private?
*Gerry Mooney, Open University*

Why have an essay on public and private ownership in a book on poverty? Primarily because privatisation impacts unevenly on different groups in the population. Among the affluent, privatisation may have opened up more opportunities and promoted choice, but for the poorest and most disadvantaged sections of Scottish society the experience has been very different. Take, for example, the poor condition of public transport in Scotland today. Not only have fares on the buses and railways risen well beyond the rate of inflation in recent years, but disadvantaged localities across the country find themselves increasingly cut off from public transport provision as private companies deem certain routes – *and groups* – unprofitable.

In this essay the terms public and private refer to the debate surrounding different forms of involvement of the private sector in the day-to-day organisation, shape and delivery of public services.[1]

## Private finance initiative and public private partnerships

Opening up the public sector to increasing penetration by for-profit companies was a clear objective of successive Conservative governments. Many utilities such as gas, electricity and transport were privatised. Other public services were subject to competitive tendering in the 'open market'.

Increased involvement of the private sector is also central to the New Labour Government's wider strategies of '*modernising*' the public sector and '*reforming*' the welfare state. The private sector, it is argued, has a central role in providing *quality*, *value for money* services, and in meeting the needs of the *consumers* of public services.

> 'Public private partnerships are all about negotiating deals that are good for both sides... In that, the public interest shares an absolute identity of inter-

est with private financiers whose return on investment will depend on services being delivered to (specified) standards.'[2]

The Government favours the use of the private finance initiative (PFI) and public private partnerships (PPPs). PFI was introduced in 1992 by the Conservative Government and adopted and expanded by the Labour Government. The schemes are seen as a way of improving the infrastructure of the country without increasing the public debt. PFI schemes usually involve large capital projects such as the building and maintaining hospitals or schools. In a PFI contract a private company is responsible for the financing, building and operating of a project for specified period of time, usually about 30 years (although the period varies). At the end of the period the project can revert back to public ownership. Performance targets are set and companies will be paid less if they do not meet them.

PPPs involve the use of private companies to provide public services such refuse collection. The Government argues that: 'while it is against full-scale privatisation...it does not matter who provides public services (it could be public, private or voluntary sector) so long as it is efficient, responsive and of good quality'.[3] PPPs providers operate in prisons, residential homes, schools and hospitals. PFI/PPPs represent some of the most controversial policies being pursued by both the Westminster and Holyrood governments.[4]

## Prudence

The increased use of PFI/PPPs are explained by the Government as a prudential measure to prevent the growth of the 'burden of public debt'. However under the Chancellor's self-imposed Treasury rules, public sector debt is to be limited to 40 per cent of GDP (gross domestic product). But the most recent figures for 2001 show it lies at only 32 per cent, providing considerable scope for massive investment in the social and public infrastructure of contemporary Scotland. Public spending today remains below that of the early 1990s and the likelihood is that it will remain under strict control for the near future. In this context local authorities, health boards, housing associations etc. have few options but to accept PFI or PPPs arrangements.

## Privatisation and its effects

The legacies of the privatisation programmes in the 1980s and 1990s can be seen in many areas today. For example, it has been widely recorded that the differential charges for gas and electricity see poor people paying more than those on direct debit schemes. Pre-payment methods, such as electricity cards, are no longer cross-subsidised by other payment methods as the utility companies strive to attract more affluent consumers. Martin Fitch argues that although prices for some staples, such as gas and electricity, have been reduced in real terms, the poor continue to pay more for such services, contributing to a widening gulf between themselves and more affluent groups.[5]

In recent years there has been a steady withdrawal of some privately provided services in disadvantaged localities across the country. For example, choice in relation to food retailing (especially in relation to fresh produce) is much more limited in poorer localities. Similarly, privatisation of the Post Office is likely to have a detrimental effect in poor and rural areas where branch closures are likely to feature strongly. Speak and Graham note that 'generally the poorer the access to a service, the more it costs' – and such costs are multiplied when services are 'restructured'.[6]

## Accountability

A major problem with PPPs is that the contracts are extremely complex and not open to public scrutiny. A report on PPPs by the Institute for Public Policy Research[7] noted that the PPPs should be more accountable to the public. The report recommended that PFI projects should be brought under the same mandatory framework for disclosing information as the NHS; and that the National Audit Office should have statutory authority to examine information on all significant public contracts. PFI/PPPs represent a kind of hire purchase or credit card finance scheme. 'Build now, pay later' may appear attractive to some now, but it will all have to be repaid at great cost in the future, using resources that would be better spent in improving public sector provision.

## What is the future likely to hold?

In twenty to thirty years' time, many of the PFI and PPP projects signed in recent times will be coming to an end. What is the future likely to hold? The New Labour governments in London and the Scottish Executive have made it clear that they will put 'investment before ideology' and that 'what matters is what works'. But this leaves unanswered the key questions: 'working for whom' and 'when'? What is clear from the privatisation programmes under both past and present governments is that what works for private companies does not unquestionably work for those on the receiving end, either as customers or as frontline workers. One of the central arguments of Conservative governments in defence of privatisation was that it would enhance choice. But choice costs money and the evidence from studies of privatisation is that far from increasing choice, the options open to poor people and in poor localities are becoming more and more limited.

The privatisation of public services marks the changing of the relationship between the individual and the state. The state's role has changed from deliverer of public services to that of enabler. There is an emerging *corporate welfare* in Britain; while this has yet to reach the levels attained in the United States, none-the-less the signs are there for all to see as companies compete to 'cherry-pick' areas of the public sector and welfare state for the maximum profit.

Ultimately the debate surrounding PFI/PPPs is not only about money or resources; it is also about accountability, democratic control and power. It is about wages, conditions of work, security of employment and the capacity of the public sector and welfare state to meet the needs of the poorest groups in society.

### Notes

1   G Mooney, 'New Labour and Managerialism: privatising the welfare state?' in M Lavalette and A Pratt (eds), *Social Policy: a conceptual and theoretical introduction*, Sage, 2001

2   Treasury Taskforce, *Partnerships for Prosperity: the private finance initiative*, The Treasury, 1997

3   P Butler, *The Guardian*, 25 June 2001

4   N Davies, *The School Report*, Vintage, 2000; and G Monbiot, *Captive State*, MacMillan, 2000

5   M Fitch, 'Does Public Utilities Mean Anything Any More?' *Poverty*, 108, Child Poverty Action Group, 2001

6   S Speak and S Graham, *Service not Included: social implications of private sector restructuring in marginalised neighbourhoods*, The Policy Press/Joseph Rowntree Foundation, 2000

7   *The Guardian*, 25 June 2001

# Fifteen

# The effects of poverty on early education – findings from the Early Intervention Programme in Scotland

*Linda Croxford, Centre for Educational Sociology, University of Edinburgh*

## Introduction

Poverty has a negative effect on children's learning before they start school and throughout their school careers. Children from socio-economically disadvantaged backgrounds start school with relatively low pre-reading skills and make less progress in reading in the early years of schooling;[1] they may suffer early experience of failure and low self-esteem compared with their more advantaged peers. Consequently, the early years of schooling have been identified as the most important time for interventions to address educational disadvantage.[2]

The Early Intervention Programme (EIP) in Scotland is a government-funded initiative started in 1997 with the aim of strengthening education in the early years. Initially the EIP emphasised the objective: 'to overcome by intervention the disadvantages and inequalities of social and domestic background, and to help all children to reach or exceed a minimum level of performance – in language and number especially – by Primary 3'.[3] However, the programme has been subsumed within policies to raise overall standards of achievement, and this has led to a change in emphasis. Research shows that overall levels of reading attainment in Primary 3 had risen dramatically by 2000, but the gap between advantaged and disadvantaged pupils had not been diminished.[4] This suggests that there may be inherent tensions in the competing priorities between raising standards and addressing inequality.

Nevertheless, there were successful interventions introduced as part of the EIP. This essay outlines some of the lessons that were learnt, and suggests that there needs to be a stronger focus on addressing the effects of poverty on early education.

## Background to early intervention

The EIP was influenced by evidence of successful programmes in the USA, and a pilot project in the Pilton area of Edinburgh. From the USA there is evidence of successful strategies targeted at socio-economic disadvantage in pre-school and the early years of primary schooling.[5] The most significant findings were:

- Quality early care and education programmes have proven effectiveness in improving the developmental outcomes of low-income and disadvantaged children.
- Quality matters, and is particularly important for children from low-income families.
- While parent-focused home visiting/parent education programmes have provided some benefits for parents, these have not translated into significantly improved outcomes for children.

Longitudinal studies of pupils included in the US Perry Pre-school project found significant measured success in terms of adult life changes such as lower delinquency, lower single parenthood and lower unemployment; a cost-benefit analysis found that for every $1 spent an estimated $7.16 was saved in lower public expenditure for welfare, education and other services.[6]

The Pilton project developed an approach to early intervention in Scotland, focusing on four schools in Edinburgh that served areas of multiple deprivation in which the children were seen to be at particular educational risk. The main thrust was an intensive staff development programme that concentrated on the explicit teaching of reading skills in Primary 1, 2 and 3, learning support for pupils who were at risk of failure, a form of reading recovery (an intensive remedial programme), the provision of nursery nurses and home-link staff. The results of the initiative, in

terms of the rise in average reading scores and reduction in the proportion of pupils who could not read in Primary 2, were remarkable.
Nevertheless it appeared that the most disadvantaged children did not
gain as much in attainment as their peers, and this was due in part to poor
attendance and persistent lateness.[7]

## Varied approaches to early intervention

Responsibility for deciding how early intervention should be implemented
in Scotland was devolved to local authorities. Each authority was free to
decide the balance of intervention activities within its schools, and was
responsible for their evaluation. This led to a very varied pattern of
approaches to early intervention, which is in contrast to the prescriptive
approach taken in England, where there is a national literacy hour. Some
local authorities followed the model provided by the Pilton project and
focused early intervention in a few schools in areas of multiple deprivation;
others included a high proportion of schools in the programme. In all areas
there was a strong emphasis on staff development and the development
of improved methods of teaching and learning. Literacy was the main
focus in the initial stages, and initiatives addressing numeracy took longer
to start.[8]

Analysis of the impact of EIP on pupils' reading scores found positive effects from a number of strategies:

- focus of resources on a small number of schools serving areas with
  high levels of deprivation;
- reading recovery;
- home-link support.

## Focus in schools serving areas with high levels of deprivation

Patterns of socially-segregated housing in towns and cities have led to
school systems in which some schools cater for large numbers of pupils
from disadvantaged backgrounds. Children's attitudes, behaviour and
learning are strongly influenced by their peers, and schools in areas of

deprivation suffer a social context in which the majority of pupils have low baseline attainment, low academic goals and it is difficult to raise pupils' aspirations and attainment.

The findings of the EIP, and the earlier Pilton project, are encouraging because they indicate that a real difference can be made to children's learning in areas of multiple deprivation. The impact of early intervention was more significant in local authorities which concentrated resources (including additional teachers, learning support and psychological services) in a small number of schools with high levels of deprivation, than in local authorities which spread resources thinly over all schools. Local authorities have difficult decisions to make concerning the allocation of resources between schools. There may be individual pupils underachieving in all schools. However, the evaluation of the EIP suggests that if the links between poverty and education are to be addressed there is need for greater concentration of support for pupils in schools with high levels of deprivation.

## Reading recovery

Reading recovery is an intensive system of individual tuition in reading, developed by Clay.[9] It has been found particularly successful in improving the reading of pupils from disadvantaged backgrounds, and a longitudinal evaluation of reading recovery in South East England found the improvement to be evident five years after the intervention took place. The researchers concluded that:

> 'Targeting intervention directly at poor children offers a viable strategy for tackling illiteracy among children from the most deprived social groups.'[10]

Reading recovery is a relatively high-cost intervention because it involves one-to-one tuition of pupils for 30 minutes daily over an average of 20 weeks. There is additional investment in specialised teacher training, and teaching materials. Nevertheless, the evaluators argued that the investment is cost-effective, and suggest that:

- children with reading difficulties are expensive to educate whether or not they get a specific intervention;
- for certain sub-groups of children, those who were very poor readers

at six and those on free school meals, reading recovery offers better value for money than existing provision.

## Home-link support

Parents and families have an important role in children's education, particularly with respect to providing encouragement for learning.[12] In many cases parents in poverty may themselves have had unhappy or unsuccessful experiences of schooling which make them less confident in their dealings with schools. Home-link teachers work between the parents and schools, and gain an understanding and appreciation of both perspectives, in order to help the parents to support their child's learning. The home-link teachers use a number of approaches to engage parents in the education of their children, including the development of early learning and adult learning initiatives. They also communicate the parents' views to the schools.

## Conclusions

The effect of poverty in perpetuating educational disadvantage appears a very long-standing and intractable problem. It has long been believed that education is a means for reducing social inequality, but in fact pupils who start school with socio-economic and educational disadvantages make less progress than their more advantaged peers, and thus the gap between advantaged and disadvantaged widens in the course of school careers. Educational attainment is the key factor predicting young people's future career opportunities and life chances; young people who leave school with low levels of educational attainment are far more likely to suffer periodic unemployment than those with higher attainment.[13] Others have argued:

> 'Children who have reading difficulties in our society suffer. As adults they are disadvantaged and may cost society dear. Both on the grounds of compassion and common sense the prevention of reading difficulties in children must be a priority.'[14]

The early years of schooling, including the pre-school years, have been identified as the most beneficial time to address educational dis–advantage. In areas of deprivation the provision of high quality nursery education is vital, and parents should be encouraged to keep children at nursery for an extra year rather than starting primary school too soon.

The EIP in Scotland, as well as research elsewhere, has indicated that appropriate, concentrated interventions can make a difference in improving the learning of pupils from disadvantaged backgrounds. However, such interventions require considerable resources including one-to-one tuition over sustained periods, and a focus of resources in the most disadvantaged schools. Home-link support is a further valuable means of supporting the learning of children from disadvantaged backgrounds.

The EIP in Scotland was initially funded by the Scottish Executive for a three-year period, which was subsequently extended to five years. Evidence from the evaluation of the programme suggests that there is continuing need for investment by the Scottish Executive in early years education. The importance of such investment is especially great in areas of multiple deprivation. If the Scottish Executive is serious in its aim of social justice it is vital that this investment is made in the education of young children in order to try to prevent further disadvantage.

## Notes

1   L Croxford, *Inequality in the First Year of Primary School*, CES Briefing No16, CES, University of Edinburgh, 1999

2   H Fraser, A MacDougall, A Pirrie and L Croxford, *National Evaluation of the Early Intervention Programme: final report*, Report to the Scottish Executive Education Department, University of Edinburgh, 2001

3   Scottish Office, *Improving Achievements in Scottish Schools*, Para 1.2, The Stationery Office, 1996

4   See note 2

5   H Fraser, *Early Intervention: a literature review, a research review for the SOEID*, published online at www.scotland.gov.uk, 1997

6   National Association of Child Advocates, *Making Investments in Young Children: what research on early care and education tells us*, published online at www.childadvocacy.org, 2000

7   See note 2

8   See note 2

9   M M Clay, *The Early Detection of Reading Difficulties*, Heinemann, 1985

10  J Hurry and K Sylva, *SCAA Evaluation of Interventions for Children with Reading*

*Difficulties: summary of five-year study,* Institute of Education, London University, 1997

11 See note 10

12 L Tett, D Caddell, J Crowther and P O'Hara, 'Parents and Schools: partnerships in early primary education', *Scottish Educational Review*, 33(1), 2001, pp48-58

13 A Biggart, *Gender and Low Achievement*, CES, University of Edinburgh, 2000

14 K Sylva and J Hurry, *The Effectiveness of Reading Recovery and Phonological Training for Children with Reading Problems*, report prepared for School Curriculum and Assessment Authority London, Thomas Coram Research, 1995

# Sixteen

# Health policy in Scotland since 1997 and its impact on poverty

*Sue Laughlin*

The association between poverty and poor health is now largely incontrovertible but the relationship is a complex one. Firstly, the impact in different countries is variable depending on the relative levels of inequality between the least and most affluent members of their populations.[1] This suggests that low income is not an absolute arbiter of poor health but that the experience of powerlessness, exclusion and discrimination has a profound effect through various psychological and physiological mechanisms.

Secondly, poverty affects the health of women and men in different ways highlighting the significance of gender as a variable. For women, the impact of lower social class is particularly evident for non-psychotic mental health problems such as depression and for men, there is a greater incidence of drug and alcohol problems. Lastly, it is also the case that the interaction works both ways; poor health can lead to poverty by limiting access to the labour market.

Scotland has one of the highest levels of poor health and premature death in Europe for both women and men. It is therefore important to assess the extent to which the health issues relating to poverty have been addressed in Scotland over the past five years. To do so effectively it is necessary to consider health policy and planning as well as what has been described as healthy public policy.[2] This essay will, however, focus on the former because of the nature of its aspirations.

Since 1997, there has been a marked shift in the analysis underpinning health policy and in its avowed aims. Under the auspices of the Scottish Office, a public health Green Paper in 1998[3] and its subsequent White Paper, *Towards a Healthier Scotland* in 1999[4] highlighted health inequalities as a priority and indicated a new-found acknowledgement of the need to tackle people's life circumstances. This was followed in late 2000 by *Our National Health: a plan for action, a plan for change*, the first major post-devolution statement, in which poverty was recognised explicitly as a key determinant of poor health:

> 'To create a healthier Scotland, we have to tackle poverty and the root causes of ill health which persist in the life circumstances of too many in Scotland… Poverty, poor housing, homelessness and the lack of educational and economic opportunity are the root causes of major inequalities in health in Scotland. We must fight the causes of illness as well as illness itself.'[5]

The plan indicates that addressing poverty and its link to health will be carried out by 'bringing different agencies together, with the NHS, to tackle the wide range of life circumstances that contribute to ill health'. From 2002 it is incumbent on health boards, which themselves have been reorganised to facilitate greater strategic planning in concert with NHS trusts, to produce local health plans with their local authority partners and for local authorities to develop their role as public health organisations. NHS boards are tasked with the responsibility of identifying the action they are taking to tackle homelessness and reduce inequalities and are held accountable to this via the performance assessment framework.

Further to this broad strategic framework, *Our National Health* makes commitments to initiatives aimed at supporting health improvement in communities, families and individuals. One hundred million pounds is being made available over four years as the Health Improvement Fund and NHS health boards and local authorities are being instructed to work together to route money to local communities, with a particular emphasis on social inclusion partnership areas. A range of healthy living centres are also being introduced, supported by £34.5 million from the New Opportunities Fund.

Despite this encouraging trend, there remain a number of paradoxes at the heart of health policy making which militate against reducing significantly the levels of poverty-related poor health. Firstly, despite the importance of addressing the determinants of poor health, it is expected that the health service will take the lead role in addressing health inequalities with local healthcare co-operatives (partnerships of general practices) identified to play a lead role in steering this agenda.

The health service, however, is constructed upon a model of understanding which recognises the manifestation of poor health but not its causes. As such it is conceptually ill-suited to take the lead in identifying solutions. It is also still the case that the majority of resources earmarked for health are targeted at the provision of health care, the much vaunted Health Improvement Fund accounting for much less than 0.01 per cent of the total budget allocation to the health service in Scotland in 2000/01. Significantly, there is no onus on the health service to adopt a gender perspective in its work despite the health effects of poverty manifesting themselves differently in women and men.

Where the health service could make a major difference in the patient's experience of ill health, there has been little or no pressure for 'improving the delivery of health care so that the diagnosis and management of health problems incorporates understanding of the social, as well as biological, factors which influence the reasons that people present to the health service, or for improving the interaction between professional and client'.[6] This omission is particularly important for those with poverty-related ill health and who use the health service the most, as it can affect the appropriateness or effectiveness of the care received.

The second paradox is the emphasis on changing the behaviours or lifestyles of individuals, especially those with the poorest health, or on addressing the outcomes of poverty-related ill health. A key plank of the public health White Paper, endorsed further by *Our National Health*, has been the funding of four demonstration projects aimed at improving children's health, improving sexual health, and reducing the incidence of heart disease and cancer. In all of these programmes, the primary emphasis has been placed on addressing health-limiting behaviour such as poor parenting, risky sexual behaviour, poor diet and lack of exercise. While it is often or exclusively poor people who are being targeted, the issue of their poverty only exists off-stage.

In its progress report following the first year of *Our National Health*, the Scottish Executive makes claim to 14 key outcomes of success.[7] Top of the list is 'an additional £128 million to tackle drug misuse – the biggest programme of anti-drugs initiatives ever implemented in Scotland' but it also includes three initiatives targeting dental health or improved dental services, increasing the availability of nicotine replacement therapy and providing healthy tuck shops in schools. Laudable as these initiatives appear to be, closer inspection reveals that they too are of a short-term nature, professionally driven, do little to articulate or address the experience of poverty and leave the causes of poverty untouched.

In 2002, the inhabitants of Scotland are still the sick women and men of Western Europe. The policy framework for making radical changes is at a crossroads and it is unclear whether a new direction will emerge. Some attempts have been made to situate health within economic and social regeneration through the social justice agenda. This essay has attempted to show however that the main assumptions for improving health have been misplaced. The leadership role given to the NHS is inappropriate because it is still underpinned by the powerful conceptual models of medicine. Providing poor individuals and poor communities with opportunities to change their lifestyles and cope with their poor health arguably may help to ameliorate some of the effects of poverty. Overall, the poor health statistics are unlikely to improve without addressing the causes of poverty and structural inequality.

## Notes

1 For example, R Wilkinson, *Unhealthy Societies: the afflictions of inequality*, Routledge, 1996

2 A Cook (ed), *Promise and Practice: will government policy improve our health*, Healthy Public Policy Network, Scottish Council Foundation, 2000

3 Scottish Office, *Working Together for a Healthier Scotland*, The Stationery Office, 1998

4 Scottish Office, *Towards a Healthier Scotland*, The Stationery Office, 1999

5 Scottish Executive, *Our National Health: a plan for action, a plan for change*, The Stationery Office, 2000

6 Scottish Executive, *Our National Health: delivering change*, The Stationery Office, 2001

7 R Ilett and S Laughlin, 'Modernising Health: the paradoxes at the heart of policymaking', in G Hassan and C Warhurst (eds), *A Different Future: a moderniser's guide to Scotland*, Centre for Scottish Public Policy/The Big Issue in Scotland, 1999

# Section four
# Conclusions

# Seventeen
# **Continuities and contradictions**

In this fourth edition of our book we provide a brief survey of poverty in Scotland and a critical review of policies and practices at the start of a new century. Editing the book provided a valuable opportunity to update figures, and make use of the varied range of new sources of data on poverty in Scotland that have become available since devolution, as well as to gather views on the impact of Westminster and Holyrood-based policy on the causes and effects of poverty.

The review of statistical material highlights the continuities as well as changes since we last visited the issue. Significant among these are the developments in the ongoing discussion of what poverty means, and how it can be measured and analysed. The policy essays examine a range of current anti-poverty measures, and focus on both the successes and concerns for Scotland and the UK. Overall the book highlights the growing recognition that poverty is a problem requiring careful analysis by policy makers if it is to be tackled in an effective way. In our conclusion we consider briefly some of the underlying issues raised by the new data and the policy essays in this book.

## **Recognising the problem**

During most of the 1980s and well into the 1990s there was a popular denial of poverty. The Child Poverty Action Group in its third edition of *Poverty: the facts* summed up the prevailing views:

> 'Poverty is a term which is rarely heard on the lips of policy makers...The debate...has been characterised by bland euphemisms...terms which obscure the reality of deprivation, poverty and hardship.'[1]

This is not an accusation that can be levelled at the current government.

Since its election in 1997, the Labour Government has made it very clear that it both accepts that poverty exists and that it has reached an unacceptable level. Frequent and clear statements have been made on the need for action to tackle poverty. Further, the Government has committed itself to eradicate child poverty in twenty years. The Scottish Parliament in 1999 reaffirmed these commitments. These are bold steps for any government and have been matched by the setting of targets against which government action can be measured and held accountable. In order to tackle any problem it is necessary to recognise that it exists, and to define it: the Government has done both. Its recognition of poverty and commitment to eradicate child poverty need to be acknowledged.

## Definitions

The Government's implicit use of a relative notion of poverty and its espousal of the concept of 'social exclusion' has opened up the debate on issues and aspects of deprivation, disadvantage and discrimination: this has to be welcomed. Too often the complexity of the causes and effects of poverty have been overlooked in analysis and policy initiatives, resulting in ineffective measures. However, there is concern that use of such a wide-ranging term as social exclusion could result in obscuring its relationship with poverty. In this context it is worth stressing that:

> 'Poverty is not only about a shortage of money. It is about rights and relationships; about how people are treated and how they regard themselves; about powerlessness, exclusion and loss of dignity. Yet the lack of an adequate income is at its heart.'[2]

## Measurements

The Government is currently consulting on how child poverty should be measured. The timing of the consultation – in the wake of the latest *Households Below Average Income 2000/01*, which showed that some of the more publicised child poverty reductions targets have not been achieved – was among the less successful of the Government's public relations ventures. It is, however, part of a process undertaken by the

Government to create effective and efficient tools of poverty measurement that can be understood and supported by the public. In creating a new measurement of child poverty, the following points should be taken into account.

First, the measurement cannot be based solely nor mainly on government indicators. Such indicators show the success or failure of Government policy and practice; these are not necessarily identical with poverty. There is also the temptation to publicise only the successful initiatives. Second, while indicators of social exclusion, inclusion and well-being help to provide a fuller picture of poverty, it should be noted that there are many other reasons, such as discrimination or lack of well-being, for example. It is important, therefore, that measurements of poverty are not swamped by more 'media-friendly' indicators. Third, a relative income threshold must be central, as this reinforces the fact that poverty is relative. Fourth, the measurement should take into account issues of adequacy. There is a need for a 'safety margin rather than a minimalist drawing of lines'.[3] Above all, independent, robust and clear measurements are needed to maintain public confidence and support.

## Work

Employment is the key tool in the Government's anti-poverty strategy. Enabling people to find work and ensuring that work pays will, in the Government's view, help people out of poverty and reduce the social security bill. The Government has widened the scope of work-based anti-poverty strategies and undertaken a number of initiatives to deal with unemployment and economic inactivity, and to make work pay. However, basic problems of the availability and sustainability of jobs remain. Despite government efforts to attract investors, the availability of jobs varies across the country. Moreover, given the underlying volatility of the markets, fewer and fewer jobs are really secure. A major problem with current strategy is that while the Government is strongly committed to increasing *employability* – that is, getting people job-ready – on the evidence in this book this is clearly not enough. But the Government shows little inclination to become involved in the creation of jobs. It is a contradiction that is likely to prove a continuing impediment to efforts to reduce poverty.

## Low pay and social mobility

The data and the policy essays in this book suggest that, although government measures have made a difference, employment does not guarantee a route out of poverty. Instead, too many people 'grapple with the insecurities and frustrations associated with spells of unemployment interspersed with low-paid work. Such work patterns taint the present with poverty and offer no respite for the future'.[4]

The current strategy to combat this cycle is to support people through training and education and help them to move out of low-paid, low-status jobs. But progression on the employment ladder cannot be guaranteed: 'without investment to provide real jobs, improved training and skills may simply equip individuals for a competitive struggle for employment in which some must lose'.[5] More importantly, there is an underlying assumption that the low-paid low-status jobs are valueless. Yet the cooking, cleaning, caring and general servicing carried out by millions provide both the basic infrastructure on which services, public and private, run and lucrative profits for industry. These are also the jobs most likely to be insecure and badly paid, and the ones that poorest groups are most encouraged to take. Unless this work is properly valued, we will not do much to eradicate poverty.

Currently, 'work pays' because of top-up in-work benefits. It may be that, as a society, we believe that it is better for people to be in employment than not, even if the state has to subsidise them. But there needs to be a level of honesty about the situation, because it is not just the poor who are benefiting: the result of such a strategy is that the state – and the taxpayer – are subsiding low-paying employers. Such a strategy will prove very expensive, and in the long run it will be more socially and economically effective to increase the minimum wage and provide for it to be independently assessed and regularly uprated.

All contributors agree that paid employment is an integral part of any anti-poverty strategy, although not the whole solution. But they note that employment is insecure, that many in employment are poor, that many cannot find work and that there will always be people who cannot work because of illness, age or caring responsibilities. Successful anti-poverty polices must take account of these different issues.

## Social security

The reform of the social security system remains central to the Government's poverty-reduction strategies, even if its plan for large-scale reform has given way to smaller incremental change. There have been a number of radical and innovative changes such as the greater use of tax credits. Our contributors note that the main focus of benefit changes has been to help the transition from welfare to work. There is recognition of the real efforts made to address some of the problems of benefit traps. But there is also concern at the increasing use of sanctions and a degree of uncertainty on how the new tax credit schemes will work out. The verdict, overall, is that there is now more support for those in employment and those moving into work, but much less is being done for those not in employment, and there is still little recognition of unpaid work.

The Government aims to create a social security system for the twenty-first century, but the structure remains embedded in the past. In particular, the persistence of the distinction between deserving and undeserving poor, and the principle of 'less eligibility' whereby state relief and the conditions to receive it are always worse than the worst paid job. These are principles that have influenced state provision since the time of the Poor Laws, and continue to do so. Common fears that people are being weaned off the work ethic by dependency on benefits, or that they are getting something they do not deserve, still underlie much of the debate on social security. While governments decide and implement policy, it needs to be recognised that policies often reflect ambivalent social attitudes. For example, the British Social Attitudes Survey showed that while two out three people recognised the existence of poverty, one in four said people were poor through their own fault.

Reform of the social security system is necessary: it is not, and should not be, seen as the sole remedy for poverty. Neither should it, as it too often does, create stigma, increase inequality and trap people in poverty. Britain needs a just and adequate social security system that assists people in poverty, helps people out of poverty, and is a crucial element in strategies to prevent poverty.

## Polarisation

Several contributors in Section 3 have referred to the polarisation between some communities and groups: this is a matter for concern. There is a tendency by governments and the media to focus on particular groups, communities or localities as embodying all the problems of poverty. Targeted policies are seen to be the solution to the problems. A result of this strategy is that groups and communities increasingly see themselves in competition for resources. The focus is on 'who is getting what?' and 'why are they getting it and not us?' Media campaigns seek to establish not just *need* but the *worth* of the groups and communities receiving funds, thereby exacerbating tensions. Adverse local reaction to the incoming refugees in Glasgow's Sighthill, and the racial tensions in Burnley in 2001, has shown that the problem is wide spread.

It is vital therefore that links between social justice policies and equality strategies are made explicit and that the value of, and need for, equity for all sections of society are made clear. It needs to be recognised that policies targeted on particular groups or communities are necessary. However, they may not have much effect on reducing total poverty, and they can increase social tensions. A mix of universal and targeted policies is therefore needed to combat poverty and discrimination. Media 'scare stories' need to be quickly rebutted, and accurate information widely circulated. This is a worthwhile job for the Government's publicity machine.

## Westminster and Holyrood

There were hopes in Scotland that devolution would bring locally-appropriate policy initiatives. As the essays in Section 3 show, there are policies being followed by the Scottish Parliament that are different from those being followed by Westminster. Examples are: the arrangements for students and higher education finance; the funding of long-term care of the elderly; and (to a lesser extent) the social inclusion/social inclusion partnerships programme. However the differences are so far fairly limited, and tend to reflect pre-existing institutional and organisational differences. Generally, policies on poverty, inequality and social inclusion/exclusion in Scotland and Britain continue to show strong similarities.[6]

Our contributors' reviews of UK and Scottish anti-poverty policy tackle this very issue. In discussing matters such as the effect of the minimum wage, or the plight of asylum seekers, contributors generally argue that the powers of the Scottish Executive are limited. But the importance of 'joining up' policies and developing effective and more explicit relationships between the London and Edinburgh administrations is widely noted.

## Inequality

The data in Section 2 and the essays in Section 3 highlight the continuing growth of inequality. Increasing affluence is not being experienced by all. Deepening inequality marginalises and excludes the poor, and fosters the social isolationism of the rich. One of the main factors in the growth of poverty in the 1980s and 1990s was the redistribution of resources from the least well off to the better off. Current anti-poverty policies do not appear to take account of these facts. Issues of power and privilege are thus avoided or obscured. A successful anti-poverty strategy must address the issues of inequality and the need for redistributive policies.

Finally, it must be recognised that the eradication of poverty is not a one-off venture. The causes of poverty are complex and have deep roots. In order to eradicate poverty we have both to end it and to ensure it does not resurface. The eradication of poverty therefore cannot depend only on the commitment of a particular government. Governments come and go. Enduring institutions and mechanisms are required: adequate benefits, a decent minimum wage and universal public services; but in addition, there needs to be a strong and continuing commitment from society as a whole. Important steps towards eradication of poverty have been taken, but a great deal more still needs to be done.

### Notes

1   C Oppenheim and L Harker, *Poverty: the facts*, Child Poverty Action Group, 1996

2   The Report of the Archbishop of Canterbury's Commission on Urban Priority Areas, *Faith in the City: a call for action by churches and nation*, Church House, 1985

3   A Sinfield, *Response to the Department for Work and Pensions Consultation Document on Measuring Child Poverty*, 2002

4 Oppenheim, *Poverty: the facts*, Child Poverty Action Group, 1993

5 R Levitas, *The Inclusive Society? Social Exclusion and New Labour*, Macmillan, 1998

6 G Mooney and C Johnstone, 'Poverty and Inequality in Scotland', *Critical Social Policy*, Vol 20:2, 2000

# Appendix one
# Suggestions for further reading

## On poverty, social exclusion and inequality:

P Beresford *et al*, *Poverty First Hand: poor people speak for themselves*, Child Poverty Action Group, 1999

U Brown and D Phillips (eds), *Even the Tatties Have Batter: free nutritious meals for all children in Scotland*, Child Poverty Action Group Scotland, 2002

D Byrne, *Social Exclusion*, Open University Press, 1999.

*Poverty in Dundee: an account of people's views and experiences*, Dundee Anti-Poverty Forum, May 2002

B Ehrenreich, *Nickel and Dimed*, Granta, 2001

M Howard *et al*, *Poverty: the facts*, Child Poverty Action Group, 2001

J Hills, J Le Grand and D Piachaud, *Understanding Social Exclusion*, CASE, Open University Press, 2002

R Levitas, *The Inclusive Society? Social exclusion and New Labour* MacMillan, 1998

T Novak, *Rich and Poor*, South Street Press, 2001

C Pantazis (ed), *Tackling Inequalities*, The Policy Press, 2000

J Percy-Smith (ed), *Policy Responses to Social Exclusion*, Open University Press, 2000

M Rahman, G Palmer and P Kenway, *Monitoring Poverty and Social Exclusion*, New Policy Institute/Joseph Rowntree Foundation, 2001

J Seymour (ed) *Poverty in Plenty: a human development report for the UK*, Earthscan/United Nations, 2000

M Shaw *et al*, *The Widening Gap: health inequalities and policy in Britain*, The Policy Press, 1999

*Dear Sir William: letters to the father of the welfare state*, Scottish Poverty Information Unit

R Walker (ed) *Ending Child Poverty*, The Policy Press, 1999

## On social policy and recent developments in welfare in Britain:

J Clarke, S Gewirtz and E McLaughlin (eds), *New Managerialism, New Welfare?* Sage/The Open University, 2000

I Ferguson, M Lavalette and G Mooney, *Rethinking Welfare: a critical discussion*, Sage, 2002

C Jones and T Novak, *Poverty, Welfare and the Disciplinary State*, Routledge, 1999

M Powell (ed), *New Labour, New Welfare State?* The Policy Press, 1999

## On 'post-devolutionary' Scotland:

*Out of the Ordinary: the power of ambition in an uncertain world*, The Scottish Council Foundation, 2001

J Curtice *et al* (eds), *New Scotland, New Society?* Polygon, 2002

G Hassan and C Warhurst (eds) *A Different Future*, Centre for Scottish Public Policy/The Big Issue in Scotland, 1999

L Paterson *et al*, *New Scotland, New Politics?* Edinburgh University Press, 2001

## General:

N Davies, *The School Report*, Vintage 2000

J Harding, *The Uninvited: refugees at the rich man's gate*, Profile Books, 2000

W Hutton, *The World We're In*, Little Brown, 2002

G Monbiot, *Captive State*, MacMillan, 2000

S P Savage and R Atkinson (eds), *Public Policy Under Blair*, Palgrave, 2001

P Toynbee and D Walker, *Did Things Get Better? An audit of Labour's successes and failures*, Penguin, 2001

## Journals and periodicals:

The following journals and periodicals (an increasing number of which can be sampled via websites) are a good source of information and material on current/recent developments in social and welfare policy in general, and poverty/inequality in particular:

- *Alliance News* (newsletter of The Poverty Alliance)

- *Critical Social Policy*
- *Journal of Social Policy*
- *Local Economy*
- *New Economy*
- *Policy and Politics*
- *Poverty* (Child Poverty Action Group journal)
- *Scottish Affairs*
- *Social Policy and Administration*

In addition, the Social Policy Association publishes an annual *Social Policy Review* that contains essays on many different aspects of social and welfare policy both in Britain and overseas.

## Websites:

- Child Poverty Action Group: www.cpag.org.uk
- Joseph Rowntree Foundation: www.jrf.org.uk
- Institute for Public Policy Research: www.ippr.org.uk
- Lothian Anti-Poverty Alliance: www.lapa.org.uk
- New Policy Institute: www.npi.org.uk, www.poverty.org.uk
- Poverty Alliance: www.povertyalliance.org.uk
- Scottish Council Foundation: www.scottishpolicynet.org.uk

# Appendix two
## Information sources

*Annual Business Enquiry* (National Statistics)
   www.statistics.gov.uk/themes/commerce/abi
*Annual Report of the Registrar General for Scotland 2000* (General Register Office
   for Scotland)
   www.gro-scotland.gov.uk/grosweb/grosweb.nsf/pages/annrep
*Client Group Analysis* – quarterly bulletins (Department for Work and Pensions)
   www.dwp.gov.uk/asd/online.html
Department for Work and Pensions: Analytic Services Department
   www.dwp.gov.uk/asd
*Disability Briefing* (Disability Rights Commission)
   www.drc-gb.org/drc/InformationAndLegislation/Page353.asp
*Economic Trends* (National Statistics)
   www.statistics.gov.uk/statbase
*Equality in Scotland – Disabled People* (Scottish Executive)
   www.scotland.gov.uk/library3/society/equality/esd-00.asp
*Facts about Women and Men in Scotland 2002* (Equal Opportunities
   Commission)
   www.eoc.org.uk/EOCeng/dynpages/research_stats.asp
*Family Resources Survey 1999/2000* (Department for Work and Pensions)
   www.dss.gov.uk/publications/dss/2001/frs
*Family Spending 1999-2000* (National Statistics)
   www.statistics.gov.uk/statbase
General Register Office for Scotland
   www.gro-scotland.gov.uk
*Households Below Average Income 2000/01* (Department for Work and Pensions)
   www.dss.gov.uk/asd/hbai/hbai2001/contents.html
*Income Support Quarterly Statistical Enquiry, Nov 2001* (Department for Work and
   Pensions)
   www.dss.gov.uk/asd/online.html
*Income-related Benefits: estimates of take-up in 1999/2000* (Department for Work
   and Pensions)
   www.dss.gov.uk/asd/online.html
Information Services Division (ISD Online) Publications, NHS Scotland

www.show.scot.nhs.uk/isd/publications/publications.htm

Institute for Fiscal Studies

www.ifs.org.uk

*Labour Force Survey* (National Statistics)

http://www.statistics.gov.uk/themes/labour_market/lfs

*Labour Market Trends* – monthly magazine (National Statistics)

www.statistics.gov.uk/statbase

Low Pay Unit

www.lowpayunit.org.uk

*Scottish Economic Statistics 2001* (Scottish Executive)

www.scotland.gov.uk/stats/ses/ses-00m.asp

Scottish Executive Statistics

www.scotland.gov.uk/stats

*Scottish House Condition Survey* (Communities Scotland)

qb.soc.surrey.ac.uk/surveys/shcs/shcsintro.htm

Scottish Household Survey (Scottish Executive)

www.scotland.gov.uk/shs

Social Justice publications (Scottish Executive)

www.scotland.gov.uk/socialjustice/index.htm

*Social Trends 2002* (National Statistics)

www.statistics.gov.uk/statbase

Statbase (National Statistics)

www.statistics.gov.uk/statbase

*Statistical Bulletin: housing series* (Scottish Executive)

www.scotland.gov.uk/stats

Time Series Data Service (Timezone, National Statistics)

www.statistics.gov.uk/statbase/tsdintro.asp

# Appendix three
## Policy diary

| Date | Westminster/ Scottish Parliament | Legislation | Areas of interest that are included | Website |
|------|------|------|------|------|
| 1997 | Westminster | Education Act 1997 (c. 44) | • Assisted places (primary) | www.legislation. hmso.gov.uk/acts/ acts1997/ 1997044.htm |
| 1997 | Westminster | Education (Schools) Act 1997 (c. 59) | • Assisted places | www.legislation. hmso.gov.uk/acts/ acts1997/ 1997059.htm |
| 1997 | Westminster | Finance Act 1997 (c. 16) | • Excise duty<br>• Insurance premium tax<br>• Value added tax<br>• Payments and overpayments in respect of indirect taxes<br>• Income tax, corporation tax and capital gains tax<br>• Inheritance tax<br>• Stamp duty and stamp duty reserve tax | www.legislation. hmso.gov.uk/acts/ acts1997/ 1997016.htm |
| 1997 | Westminster | Finance (No. 2) Act 1997 (c. 58) | • The windfall tax<br>• Value added tax and excise duties<br>• Income tax and corporation tax | www.legislation. hmso.gov.uk/acts/ acts1997/ 1997058.htm |

| 1997 | Westminster | National Health Service (Primary Care) Act 1997 (c. 46) | • Charges for dental treatment | www.legislation. hmso.gov.uk/acts/ acts1997/ 1997046.htm |
|------|-------------|------|------|------|
| 1997 | Westminster | Social Security Administration (Fraud) Act 1997 | • Offences, penalties and overpayments | www.legislation. hmso.gov.uk/acts/ acts1997/ 1997047.htm |
| 1998 | Westminster | Community Care (Residential Accommodation) Act 1998 (c. 19) | • Consideration of a person's pension in determining provision of residential accommodation | www.legislation. hmso.gov.uk/acts/ acts1998/ 19980019.htm |
| 1998 | Westminster | Finance Act 1998 (c. 36) | • Excise duties amendments | www.legislation. hmso.gov.uk/acts/ acts1998/ 19980036.htm |
| 1998 | Westminster | Human Rights Act 1998 (c. 42) | • Re: European Convention on Human Rights | www.legislation. hmso.gov.uk/acts/ acts1998/ 19980042.htm |
| 1998 | Westminster | National Minimum Wage Act 1998 (c. 39) | • National minimum wage for workers over the compulsory school age <br>• No differences in rate for sectors/ geographical areas/ ages/occupations <br>• Secretary of State must refer to the Low Pay Commission | www.legislation. hmso.gov.uk/acts/ acts1998/ 19980039.htm |
| 1998 | Westminster | School Standards and Framework Act 1998 (c. 31) | • Changes to school and nursery provision. <br>• Education action zones | www.legislation. hmso.gov.uk/acts/ acts1998/ 19980031.htm |

| 1998 | Westminster | Social Security Act 1998 (c. 14) | • Social security provision changes<br>• Changes to rates of maternity allowance and short-term incapacity allowance<br>• Changes to discretionary payments from the social fund<br>• Power to reduce child benefit for lone parents | www.legislation. hmso.gov.uk/acts/ acts1998/ 19980014.htm |
|------|-------------|------------------------------------|----------------------------------------------------------------------------------------------------------------------------------------------------------------------------------------------------------------------------------------------|-----------------------------------------------------------|
| 1999 | Westminster | Employment Relations Act 1999 (c.26) | • Call for regulations to ensure that part-time workers are treated no less favourably than full-time workers<br>• Exclusion of eligibility to the national minimum wage for certain people | www.legislation. hmso.gov.uk/acts/ acts1999/ 19990026.htm |
| 1999 | Westminster | Finance Act 1999 (c.16) | • Introduction of children's tax credit | www.legislation. hmso.gov.uk/acts/ acts1999/ 19990016.htm |
| 1999 | Westminster | Immigration and Asylum Act 1999 (c.33) | • Support for asylum seekers (financial and otherwise) | www.legislation. hmso.gov.uk/acts/ acts1999/ 19990033.htm |
| 1999 | Westminster | Social Security Contributions (Transfer of Functions, etc.) Act 1999 (c.2) | • Amendments to decisions, appeals and payments | www.legislation. hmso.gov.uk/acts/ acts1999/ 19990002.htm |
| 1999 | Westminster | Tax Credits Act 1999 (c. 10) | • Replacement of family credit with working families' tax credit and disability working allowance with disabled person's tax credit | www.legislation. hmso.gov.uk/acts/ acts1999/ acts1999/ Replacement of |

| 1999 | Westminster | Welfare Reform and Pensions Act 1999 (c.30) | • Stakeholder pension scheme <br> • Amendments re: personal and occupational pension schemes <br> • Preservation of rights in respect of additional pensions <br> • Extension of entitlement to state maternity allowance <br> • Amendments to various benefits, including benefits for widows and widowers, jobseeker's allowance, incapacity benefits and disability benefits | www.legislation. hmso.gov.uk/acts/ acts1999/ 19990030.htm |
|------|-------------|----------------------------------------------|----------------------------------------------------------------------------------------------------------------------------------------------------------------------------------------------------------------------------------------------------------------------------------------------------------------------------------------------------------------------------------------------|-----------------------------------------------------------|
| 2000 | Scottish Parliament | Standards in Scotland's Schools etc. Act 2000 asp 6 | • Provision of education for pre-school children <br> • Grants in respect of activities relating to school education | www.scotland-legislation.hmso. gov.uk/legislation/ scotland/acts2000/ 20000006.htm |
| 2000 | Scottish Parliament | Education and Training (Scotland) Act 2000 asp 8 | • Education and training grants | www.scotland-legislation.hmso. gov.uk/legislation/ scotland/acts2000/ 20000008.htm |

| | | | | |
|---|---|---|---|---|
| 2000 | Westminster | Child Support, Pensions and Social Security Act 2000 (c.19) | • Amendments to Child Support legislation<br>• Amendments to State Pension legislation<br>• Amendments to Occupational and Personal Pension Schemes legislation<br>• Amendments to Social Security, including loss of benefit, housing benefit and council tax benefit | www.legislation. hmso.gov.uk/acts/ acts2000/ 20000019.htm |
| 2000 | Westminster | Finance Act 2000 (c.17) | • Excise duty<br>• Income tax<br>• Pension schemes | www.legislation. hmso.gov.uk/acts/ acts2000/ 20000017.htm |
| 2000 | Westminster | Warm Homes and Energy Conservation Act 2000 (c.31) | • Requirement for Secretary of State to publish and implement a strategy to reduce fuel poverty | www.legislation. hmso.gov.uk/acts/ acts2000/ 20000031.htm |
| 2001 | Scottish Parliament | Transport (Scotland) Act 2001 asp 2 | • Travel concession schemes<br>• Grants for travel-related purposes<br>• Disabled persons' transport needs | www.scotland-legislation.hmso. gov.uk/legislation/ scotland/acts2001/ 20010002.htm |
| 2001 | Scottish Parliament | Education (Graduate Endowment and Student Support) (Scotland) Act 2001 asp 6 | • Introduction of graduate endowment<br>• Amendment of financial support for students legislation | www.scotland-legislation.hmso. gov.uk/legislation/ scotland/acts2001/ 20010006.htm |

| 2001 | Scottish Parliament | Housing (Scotland) Act 2001 asp 10 | • Homelessness and allocation of housing<br>• Tenants of social landlords<br>• Right to buy<br>• Statement on fuel poverty<br>• Assistance for housing purposes<br>• Improvement grants | www.scotland-legislation.hmso.gov.uk/legislation/scotland/acts2001/20010010.htm |
|---|---|---|---|---|
| 2001 | Westminster | Finance Act 2001 c.9 | • Income tax<br>Excise duties<br>• Pension funds | www.legislation.hmso.gov.uk/acts/acts2001/20010009.htm |
| 2002 | Scottish Parliament | School Education (Amendment) (Scotland) Act 2002 asp 2 | • Amendment regarding placing requests for children under school age | www.scotland-legislation.hmso.gov.uk/legislation/scotland/acts2002/20020002.htm |
| 2002 | Scottish Parliament | Community Care and Health (Scotland) Act 2002 asp 5 | • Charging and not charging for social care | www.scotland-legislation.hmso.gov.uk/legislation/scotland/acts2002/20020005.htm |
| 2002 | Scottish Parliament | Education (Disability Strategies and Pupils' Educational Record) (Scotland) Act 2002 asp 12 | • Accessibility strategies | www.scotland-legislation.hmso.gov.uk/legislation/scotland/acts2002/20020012.htm |
| 2002 | Westminster | Homelessness Act 2002 c.7 | • Duty of local housing authority to formulate a homelessness strategy<br>• Other functions related to homelessness | www.legislation.hmso.gov.uk/acts/acts2002/20020007.htm |
| 2002 | Westminster | State Pension Credit Act 2002 c.16 | • Introduction of state pension credit | www.legislation.hmso.gov.uk/acts/acts2002/20020016.htm |